Latino Poverty in the New Century: Inequalities, Challenges and Barriers

Latino Poverty in the New Century: Inequalities, Challenges and Barriers has been co-published simultaneously as *Journal of Poverty*, Volume 4, Numbers 1/2 2000.

The *Journal of Poverty* Monographic "Separates"

Below is a list of "separates," which in serials librarianship means a special issue simultaneously published as a special journal issue or double-issue *and* as a "separate" hardbound monograph. (This is a format which we also call a "DocuSerial.")

"Separates" are published because specialized libraries or professionals may wish to purchase a specific thematic issue by itself in a format which can be separately cataloged and shelved, as opposed to purchasing the journal on an on-going basis. Faculty members may also more easily consider a "separate" for classroom adoption.

"Separates" are carefully classified separately with the major book jobbers so that the journal tie-in can be noted on new book order slips to avoid duplicate purchasing.

You may wish to visit Haworth's website at . . .

http://www.haworthpressinc.com

. . . to search our online catalog for complete tables of contents of these separates and related publications.

You may also call 1-800-HAWORTH (outside US/Canada: 607-722-5857), or Fax 1-800-895-0582 (outside US/Canada: 607-771-0012), or e-mail at:

getinfo@haworthpressinc.com

Latino Poverty in the New Century: Inequalities, Challenges and Barriers

Maria Vidal de Haymes
Keith M. Kilty
Elizabeth A. Segal
Editors

Latino Poverty in the New Century: Inequalities, Challenges and Barriers has been co-published simultaneously as *Journal of Poverty,* Volume 4, Numbers 1/2 2000.

Routledge
Taylor & Francis Group

NEW YORK AND LONDON

First Published by
The Haworth Press, Inc., 10 Alice Street, Binghamton, NY 13904-1580 USA

Transferred to Digital Printing 2011 by Routledge
270 Madison Ave, New York NY 10016
2 Park Square, Milton Park, Abingdon, Oxon, OX14 4RN

Latino Poverty in the New Century: Inequalities, Challenges and Barriers has been co-published simultaneously as *Journal of Poverty,* Volume 4, Numbers 1/2 2000.

The development, preparation, and publication of this work has been undertaken with great care. However, the publisher, employees, editors, and agents of The Haworth Press and all imprints of The Haworth Press, Inc., including The Haworth Medical Press® and the Pharmaceutical Products Press®, are not responsible for any errors contained herein or for consequences that may ensue from use of materials or information contained in this work. Opinions expressed by the author(s) are not necessarily those of The Haworth Press, Inc.

Cover illustration by Camille Hoffman.

Cover design by Thomas J. Mayshock Jr.

Cover illustrator Camille Hoffman, 13, has been drawing ever since she could hold a pencil in her hand. To her, art is life, and it goes back generations. She continues to create art to this day and hopes to become an artist as an adult.

Library of Congress Cataloging-in-Publication Data

Latino poverty in the new century : inequalities, challenges and barriers / Maria Vidal de Haymes, Keith M. Kilty, Elizabeth A. Segal, editors.
   p. cm.
   "Has been co-published simultaneously as Journal of poverty, Volume 4, Number 1/2, 2000."
   Includes bibliographical references and index.
   ISBN 0-7890-1160-3 (alk. paper)–ISBN 0-7890-1161-1 (pbk. : alk. paper)
   1. Hispanic Americans–Economic conditions–21st century. 2. Hispanic Americans–Social conditions–21st century. 3. Hispanic Americans–Politics and government–21st century. 4. Poverty–United States. 5. United States–Economic policy–21st century. 6. United States–Ethnic relations. I. De Haymes, Maria Vidal. II. Kilty, Keith M. (Keith Michael), 1946- III. Segal, Elizabeth A. IV. Journal of poverty.
   E184.S75 L3625 2000
   305.868073–dc21   00-38853

Publisher's Note
The publisher has gone to great lengths to ensure the quality of this reprint but points out that some imperfections in the original may be apparent.

ABOUT THE EDITORS

Maria Vidal de Haymes, PhD, MSW, is Associate Professor in the School of Social Work at Loyola University in Chicago. She teaches courses in the areas of social welfare policy, community organizing, and multiculturalism. She has published research concerning Latino immigrants in the U.S., child welfare policy and practice, and social work education. Dr. Vidal de Haymes has served as a consultant to numerous local and state agencies and has served on the board of several Latin community-based organizations and state agency boards. She is a member of the National Association of Social Workers, the Society for the Study of Social Problems, and the Latino Social Workers Association.

Keith M. Kilty, PhD, is Professor in the College of Social Work at Ohio State University in Columbus. He has published or presented more than 50 papers and is a member of the editorial board for the *Journal of Studies on Alcohol* and an Assistant Editor for the *Journal of Drug Issues.* Dr. Kilty is a member of the Society for the Study of Social Problems and is currently chair of its Division on Poverty, Class and Inequality. He is also a member of the National Steering Committee of the Social Welfare Action Alliance (formerly the Bertha Capen Reynolds Society) and the Vice President of the Ohio State University Chapter of the American Association of University Professors.

Elizabeth A. Segal, PhD, MSW, is Professor in the School of Social Work at Arizona State University in Tempe. She has made many presentations and conducted workshops and seminars on various issues concerning social work, and she is the author of many articles, book chapters, book reviews, proceedings, and reports. She served as a policy analyst in Washington, DC, as an American Association for the Advancement of Science Fellow. Dr. Segal is a member of the National Association of Social Workers, the Council on Social Work Education, and the Social Welfare Action Alliance (formerly the Bertha Capen Reynolds Society).

Latino Poverty in the New Century: Inequalities, Challenges and Barriers:

CONTENTS

THOUGHTS ON POVERTY AND INEQUALITY

Preface

As the United States prepares to enter a new century, Latinos are about to become the largest racial/ethnic group in the country. In the past three decades, this often neglected group has more than tripled in absolute numbers. According to *Hispanic,* a popular magazine, "At the end of the first quarter of 1999, the Hispanic population reached 31.4 million, or 11.5 percent of the total U.S. population. By mid-2002, Hispanics will become the largest minority group in the United States" (*Hispanic,* 1999, p. 18).

For most Americans, Latinos until recently were largely outside of everyday social encounters, visible mainly in the form of stereotypical characters such as Desi Arnez or Charo or the Zoot Suit riots (Rodriguez, 1997). Even now, when Hispanics can be found in any state in the country, most of the population is concentrated in five geographic areas: California, Texas, New York, Miami, and Chicago account for 73% of the total, nearly three out of four (*Hispanic,* 1999). Now, though, as the numbers increase, Latinos are an increasingly emergent entity in the American racial and ethnic landscape.

The Latino presence is felt in many ways, not the least of which is their status as an oppressed and exploited group. Inequalities abound between Latinos and the dominant Anglo society. In order for the Latino community to achieve its rightful place in this society, a wide variety of barriers and challenges must be confronted. Social policy can provide an avenue for attaining parity with Anglos, or it can serve as a mechanism for maintaining unequal status. Thus, this volume provides wide-ranging analyses of some of the pressing issues and social policies that highlight the impact of inequality and poverty of resources and opportunities. We begin with a look at various public policies, including immigration, wel-

[Haworth co-indexing entry note]: "Preface." Vidal de Haymes, Maria, Keith M. Kilty, and Elizabeth A. Segal. Co-published simultaneously in *Journal of Poverty* (The Haworth Press, Inc.) Vol. 4, No. 1/2, 2000, pp. xv-xvii; and: *Latino Poverty in the New Century: Inequalities, Challenges and Barriers* (ed: Maria Vidal de Haymes, Keith M. Kilty, and Elizabeth A. Segal) The Haworth Press, Inc., 2000, pp. xiii-xv. Single or multiple copies of this article are available for a fee from The Haworth Document Delivery Service [1-800-342-9678, 9:00 a.m. - 5:00 p.m. (EST). E-mail address: getinfo@haworthpressinc.com].

fare, and health policy. Many of these factors are interrelated. While most Hispanics are U.S. citizens by birth, many are not or have family who are not. Because of recent anti-immigrant sentiment in this country, recent changes have occurred in public welfare and health programs as well. Many of these changes are based on misunderstandings and misrepresentations about Latinos.

Other analyses in this volume focus on the structuring of extracurricular opportunities in high school as a way of keeping Latino students in school, on community organizing within Latino communities, on participation in the political process among Latino voters, and on networks and circular migration dynamics. One of the important issues that emerges from these works is the diversity within the Hispanic community. Latinos are often looked at as a monolithic group, but in fact they represent a wide variety of ethnic groups. The three largest are Mexican-American, Puerto Rican, and Cuban-American, but there are many people from the diverse societies that make up Latin America. This diversity represents a challenge to Hispanics in building coalitions among themselves as well as with other minority groups in the U.S.

In the last article, we present reactions to poverty and inequality in a more personal way, in the voices of several Latino immigrants enrolled in a U.S. citizenship class who experience inequality on a daily basis. In this piece, the students' experiences with injustice in the workplace are contrasted with the items they must memorize for the citizenship test regarding the Declaration of Independence and its premise of equality for all.

This book represents an effort to address some of the challenges facing the large and multifaceted community labeled as Hispanic. Latinos have been a part of this country since its founding. Yet for too long they have been kept outside the mainstream. Now, as Latino communities grow and their presence in American society increases, so too does the need increase to break down the barriers that keep Hispanic people from realizing their legitimate standing in this society.

This volume strives to open that discussion and recommend ways to move beyond inequality and marginalization of Latinos within the United States.

Maria Vidal de Haymes
Keith M. Kilty
Elizabeth A. Segal

REFERENCES

Hispanic. (1999). Growth trends. *Hispanic* (September), 18.

Rodriguez, C. E. (Ed.) (1997). *Latin looks: Images of Latinas and Latinos in the U.S. Media*. Boulder, CO: Westview.

Racism, Nativism, and Exclusion: Public Policy, Immigration, and the Latino Experience in the United States

Keith M. Kilty
Maria Vidal de Haymes

SUMMARY. While population growth for the Latino population has surged since the middle of this century, people of Spanish origin have been part of the American fabric since the nation's earliest days. Since the Treaty of Guadalupe Hidalgo, which ended the Mexican-American War in 1848 and ceded most of what is now the American Southwest to the United States, Hispanics in this country (whether born here or outside U.S. borders) have been affected in various ways by the exclusionary and restrictive nature of U.S. immigration laws and policies. Most Latinos are U.S. citizens (62% by birth and an additional 7% by naturalization), but those who are citizens often have family members residing in the U.S. who are not. Recently, anti-immigrant and exclusionary sentiments have surfaced once again, much of which has been focused incorrectly on Latinos. Public policy is a critical matter for minorities, who typically occupy positions toward the bottom of the social hierarchy. In this paper, we examine the impact of social policy on the lives of Hispanics, including recent immigration and border legislation, welfare

Keith M. Kilty is Professor in the College of Social Work, Ohio State University, 1947 College Road, Columbus, OH 43210.

Maria Vidal de Haymes is Associate Professor in the School of Social Work, Loyola University-Chicago, 820 N. Michigan Avenue, Chicago, IL 60611.

The authors would like to thank Steven Rosenthal for his invaluable comments on an earlier draft of the manuscript.

An earlier version of this paper was presented at the annual meeting of the Society for the Study of Social Problems, Chicago, Illinois, August 1999.

[Haworth co-indexing entry note]: "Racism, Nativism, and Exclusion: Public Policy, Immigration, and the Latino Experience in the United States." Kilty, Keith M., and Maria Vidal de Haymes. Co-published simultaneously in *Journal of Poverty* (The Haworth Press, Inc.) Vol. 4, No. 1/2, 2000, pp. 1-25; and: *Latino Poverty in the New Century: Inequalities, Challenges and Barriers* (ed: Maria Vidal de Haymes, Keith M. Kilty, and Elizabeth A. Segal) The Haworth Press, Inc., 2000, pp. 1-25. Single or multiple copies of this article are available for a fee from The Haworth Document Delivery Service [1-800-342-9678, 9:00 a.m. - 5:00 p.m. (EST). E-mail address: getinfo@haworthpressinc.com].

reform, and official language policy and educational programs. Much of the rhetoric used to justify recent policy changes and proposals is based on misperceptions, misrepresentations, and misunderstandings. *[Article copies available for a fee from The Haworth Document Delivery Service: 1-800-342-9678. E-mail address: <getinfo@haworthpressinc.com> Website: <http://www.haworthpressinc.com>]*

KEYWORDS. Racism, nativism, exclusion, immigration, Latino, Hispanic, public policy, social welfare

While people of Spanish origin predate most others of European descent in what is now the United States, the "official" count of Hispanics was quite small until recently. During the past three decades, the apparent size of the Latino population has increased dramatically. All the same, there is some difficulty in determining the exact size, much less growth, of the Hispanic population prior to 1970, since definitions of "Spanish-origin" and "Hispanic" changed from one census to another. In fact, in 1930 Mexican-Americans were identified as a separate racial category, a designation that disappeared in 1940 when they were identified by the Census Bureau as part of the white population. At that point, Hispanics, including Mexican-Americans, came to be treated as an "ethnic" category (Gibson & Lennon, 1999). It was not until the 1970 census, though, that the Census Bureau included "Hispanic" in its standard enumeration and description of the U.S. population, as well as similar, although not identical, criteria for identifying Hispanics.

In the historical census statistics, the only inclusion of "Hispanic" prior to 1970 occurred in 1940, when 1,861,400 people were enumerated, about 1.4% of the total U.S. population. Other population estimates suggest that by 1950 the numbers of Latinos more than doubled to some 4,000,000 people, about 2.7% of the population (Hraba, 1994). That increase may be partly due to the criteria used for identifying individuals as Hispanic or to the adequacy of the count at different points in time.

In more recent years, counts presumably have become more accurate. In the 1970 census, the 9,073,000 people identified as Hispanic accounted for 4.5% of the total U.S. population. In 1980, over 5,000,000 more people were counted (14,609,000), with Hispanics accounting for 6.4% of all U.S. residents. That reflected a growth rate of 61.0%. Similar increases occurred during the next decade, with 22,354,000 Hispanics counted in the 1990 census, amounting to 9.0%

of the population. The rate of growth for that period was 53.0%, rivaling that of the previous decade. According to 1996 estimates, the Hispanic population numbered 28,438,000 people at mid-decade, some 10.8% of the population (del Pinal & Singer, 1997)–about one out of every nine residents of the United States. A September 8, 1998, press release from the U.S. Census Bureau, estimated the number of Hispanics as of July 1, 1998, at 30,400,000 people, some 11.3% of the resident population. The Census Bureau projects that the Hispanic population will overtake the Black population and become the largest minority among people of color by 2010 (Day, 1996).

While population growth for the Latino population has surged since the middle of this century, it is important to recognize that, as noted earlier, people of Spanish origin have been part of the American fabric since the nation's earliest days. In fact, the oldest city in the country is St. Augustine, Florida, although Florida did not become part of the U.S. until 1819. The Latino experience in the United States actually began with the Louisiana Purchase in 1803 but was especially propelled by this country's expansionist wars of the nineteenth century, namely, the Mexican-American War (1846-1848) and the Spanish-American War (1898). In fact, at least until recent years, the bulk of the Hispanic population came about through colonialism: by the acquisition of new territory through imperialist conquest.

Because of the fact that Latinos as often as not found themselves becoming "citizens" of the U.S., willing or not, because of where they happened to live, public policy has had a profound impact on their lives. Actually, public policy is a critical matter for minorities, who typically occupy positions toward the bottom of the socioeconomic hierarchy as is the case for Hispanics in the U.S. (del Pinal & Singer, 1997). Social policy can help exploited and oppressed groups achieve their legal rights and rightful positions in a society, or it can maintain that exploitation and degradation, as the Jim Crow segregation era did for Blacks in the American South. Yet public policy is even more crucial when one's status as a "citizen" is at issue.

RACE AND ETHNICITY, IMMIGRATION, AND FEARS ABOUT POPULATION GROWTH

Much of the growth in the Latino population during the past three decades has been due to immigration. In fact, Mexico is the leading country of origin for recent immigrants to the U.S., with almost one-fourth of all current immigrants coming from that country. Over half of all legal immigration during the 1990s has been from Latin America (Martin & Midgley, 1999). But other regions of the world are still important, and 30% of immigration during the 1990s was from Asian countries. In fact, Asian immigration surpassed Latin American during the 1980s (Martin & Midgley, 1999).

During the past three decades, some 75% to 85% of immigration has come from Latin America and Asia (Martin & Midgley, 1999). As a result, this "new immigration" of the late twentieth century, now nearly a million people a year, has involved very large numbers of "people of color." Unfortunately, it has coincided with a surge of nativism and exclusionary efforts in the United States. The contemporary anti-immigrant climate, however, is nothing new; it has long historical roots. Anxieties about who "belongs here" and what the American self-image ought to be have cropped up throughout the history of this country. At various points, such fears have led to restriction and exclusion of immigrants. As Portes and Rumbaut (1996, p. 94) have noted, "Throughout the history of American immigration, a consistent thread has been the fear that the 'alien element' would somehow undermine the institutions of the country and lead it down the path of disintegration and decay."

Pat Buchanan's frenzied rhetoric about the dangers of immigration echoes sentiments from a hundred years ago. The major difference now is that Buchanan and his contemporaries can draw on past historical precedents to justify their hostility. The primary danger had already been identified by their predecessors:

> As the anti-foreign voices grew in the late nineteenth and early twentieth centuries, they found a new argument to restrict Europeans: racism. While prior objections had been based on economics, crime, health, morality, religion and fear of radical alien ideas, now the restrictionists argued that the peoples of southern and eastern Europe were distinct races who were inferior to the so-called races of northern and western Europe. (Reimers, 1998, p. 16)

As race became the focal point of the anti-immigration forces, it quickly moved beyond the inferiority of certain Europeans to include

Asians and Latin Americans as well, particularly when good economic times turned bad.

Throughout the existence of the United States, the dominant white population has used nativist and racist beliefs to support exclusion and restriction, to create the ideology of modern racism. That is, racism in America became the justification for the enslavement of African-Americans (Bennett, 1975) and the destruction of Native Americans (Drinnon, 1990). For nonwhites, including Native Americans, the nativist and racist ideas of the nineteenth century and the first part of the twentieth century allowed restrictions to be placed on their recognition as U.S. citizens, whether by birth or naturalization (Takagi, 1989).

Mexican migrant farm laborers, who were welcomed in the early years of the twentieth century, found themselves systematically rounded up and deported during the Great Depression years. In the American Southwest where many such laborers were native-born U.S. citizens, they still found themselves deported by local and state governments, under the assumption that they were Mexican by birth (Meier & Ribera, 1993; Schaefer, 1993). Yet, as Reimers (1998) notes, the economy alone was not responsible. Racism was a powerful force and came to be expressed in public policy, including the most restrictive immigration law to that point, the National Origins Act of 1924. This law took effect several years before the Great Depression and "not only barred further entries from most countries, but did so on explicitly racial considerations" (Portes & Rumbaut, 1996, pp. 162-163).

While "Hispanic" is generally identified by social scientists as an "ethnic" category rather than a "racial" one, Hispanics tend to be seen by most whites or Anglos in racial terms (i.e., in terms of skin color)–as "brown" in contrast to "black" and "red" and "yellow" and "white." According to Marger (1991, p. 280), "If there is a common theme that runs through the unique histories and experiences of the several Hispanic groups in the United States it is their intermediate ethnic status between European-American groups, on the one hand, and African Americans, on the other." As he further notes, "Perhaps the most obvious and consequential 'in-between' feature of Hispanic Americans is their racial status" (p. 281).

Since the Treaty of Gaudalupe Hidalgo, which ended the Mexican-American War in 1848 and ceded most of what is now the American Southwest to the United States, Latinos in this country–whether born here or outside U.S. borders–have been affected in various ways by the exclusionary and restrictive nature of U.S. immigration laws and policies. The impact of public policy on Latinos is not merely a function of specific immigration law, but is felt in other areas as well, where non-citizens who are Hispanic are now being targeted. In fact, most Latinos are U.S. citizens, 62% by birth and an additional 7% by naturalization (del Pinal & Singer, 1997). Yet those who are citizens often have family members residing in the U.S. who are not, and *la migra* ("immigration") is always a factor in their lives.

In this paper, we will examine the impact of public policy on the lives of Hispanics, including recent immigration legislation and border issues (e.g., militarization and the use of military patrols, increased funding of border patrols and Immigration and Naturalization Service (INS) activities, construction of physical barriers along the Mexico-U.S. border), welfare reform policy and other health and human services issues (e.g., Medicaid, food stamps), official language policy (e.g., restrictions on the language in which public documents can be printed or work-place language), and educational policy and funding (e.g., Proposition 187, bilingual education, ESL).

IMMIGRATION POLICY

Since the founding of the United States, some sixty million "immigrants" have come to this country (Martin & Midgley, 1994). The reasons leading people to emigrate vary widely, and not all so-called immigrants would necessarily identify themselves as such. According to Martin and Midgley (1994, p. 21), "The word 'immigrant' was coined around 1789 to describe an alien who voluntarily moved from one established society to another."

The numbers of people coming from other "established societies" to the U.S. have ebbed and flowed throughout our history. This ebb and flow has been affected by many conditions, including economics and war. It has also been affected by specific policies, more often than not laws intended to restrict entry into the U.S.

From Open to Closed Borders

Immigration policies for this country have varied considerably over time, ranging from relatively open and unrestricted to closed and highly restricted. Martin and Midgley (1999) identify three primary phases of immigration policy in U.S. history: a "laissez-faire" period, a period of "qualitative restrictions," and a period of "quantitative restrictions."

Martin and Midgley date the laissez-fair period from 1780 to 1875, a time when many interests actively promoted immigration to the new nation because of the need for laborers. The only major immigration legislation was the 1790 Naturalization Act, which established the conditions for becoming a naturalized citizen. There was some concern in the 1840s about immigration because of Irish and German Catholics, but this anti-immigrant sentiment did not become widespread because of other national concerns at the time; namely, slavery and eventually the Civil War.

While Martin and Midgley paint this era as relatively benign, the beginning of restrictive immigration policy actually had its origins in the Naturalization Act, which limited naturalized citizenship to whites only (Takagi, 1989). Blacks would not be recognized as citizens until after the Civil War and ratification of the Fourteenth Amendment in 1868, and Native American Indians were not granted citizenship until the Indian Citizenship Act of 1924 (Parrillo, 2000). Restrictions on citizenship for Asians continued until 1952. Furthermore, with passage of the Cable Act in 1922, white American women could even be stripped of their citizenship if they married anyone who was not eligible to become a U.S. citizen (Takagi, 1989). For nonwhites, then, the first century of the United States provided the possibility of economic opportunity but at the expense of political rights. As Takagi (1989, p. 14) so eloquently points out, "Citizenship is a prerequisite for suffrage–political power essential for groups to defend and advance their rights and interests."

The second era, one of qualitative restrictions, lasted from 1875 to 1920. According to Martin and Midgley (1999, p. 18), "The fear of foreigners led to the imposition of qualitative restrictions aimed at barring certain types of immigrants." First were convicts and prostitutes in 1875, followed by paupers and so-called mental defectives in 1882. However, racism was also one of these "qualitative restrictions." As slavery died out in the Americas, indentured laborers from Asia replaced the freed slaves on the sugar plantations of British colonies, a practice that then spread throughout the Americas in the nineteenth century (Northrup, 1995). Chinese workers were brought to the U.S. to work on the railroads, and many later became migrant farm laborers. An anti-Chinese movement in California eventually led the U.S. congress to enact the Chinese Exclusion Act of 1882, a ban on further immigration that would remain in effect until 1943 (Martin & Midgley, 1999; Takagi, 1989).

The final era, beginning in 1920 and continuing to the present, "imposed restrictions on the annual number of immigrants allowed into the United States" (Martin & Midgley, 1999, p. 19). The National Origins Act of 1924 set an annual limit of 150,000 total immigrants. However, it also established specific quotas for particular countries. Japanese immigrants, for example, were completely prohibited, while northern and western European immigrants were given sizeable numbers (Takagi, 1989). Not even those fleeing the Nazis were given any special consideration during 1930s, and many of those who were denied admittance to this country would die in Nazi labor and death camps. It was not until after the end of World War II that immigration consideration was given to refugees, through the 1948 Displaced Persons Act and the 1953 Refugee Relief Act (Takagi, 1989).

Latinos and Immigration Policy

Coercion has played an important role in enlarging not only the territory but also the population of this country. In addition to slaves who were brought to these shores from Africa, there was also "the incorporation of native American, Spanish, and French populations as the boundaries of the United States expanded westward" (Martin & Midgley, 1994, p. 21). First were the Mexicans and Native Americans living in the Southwest following the Mexican-American War and the Treaty of Guadalupe Hidalgo in 1848, and fifty years later Puerto Ricans, who became colonial subjects of the U.S. after the Spanish-American War of 1898. The absorption of Hispanics into the U.S. fabric through imperialist expansion has indelibly defined their position within this nation.

For Mexican-Americans, this absorption began with the Texas rebellion in 1835 and the annexation of Texas to the United States in 1845. At the conclusion of the Mexican-American War, Mexico lost nearly half its territory to the U.S. through the 1848 Treaty of Guadalupe Hidalgo. The U.S. acquired California, Arizona, New Mexico, Nevada, Utah, and parts of Wyoming, Colorado, Kansas, and Oklahoma. In 1854, the U.S. obtained some additional territory, including what is now southwestern New Mexico and southern Arizona (Martinez, 1996). For the residents of these lands, the Treaty of Guadalupe Hidalgo was especially important, since its provisions supposedly guaranteed property and citizenship rights. However, as del Castillo (1996, p. 7) notes, "The proponents asserted that the treaty provisions for citizenship and property rights in Articles VIII and IX would be sufficient to protect the former Mexican citizens. They were wrong: American local, state, and national courts later ruled that the provisions of the treaty could be superseded by local laws."

All the same, this annexation of what is now the southwestern region of the United States was the beginning of the American Hispanic community. In 1996, Americans of Mexican ancestry accounted for 64% of Hispanic Americans (del Pinal & Singer, 1997). While recognized as citizens, Mexican Americans found their rights and opportunities abridged from the very beginning of annexation. Many had family on both sides of the border, and the boundaries identified by the U.S. and Mexico had little meaning to those living in the region (Meier & Ribera, 1993).

For most of the twentieth century, the border has moved from relatively open to relatively closed, depending on economic circumstances. During the Great Depression, food prices fell sharply, and a surplus labor force developed, consisting of Mexicans and Mexican-Americans. This led to a massive "repatriation" program, particularly in California. According to Meier and Ribera (1993, p. 154), "The 1940 census counted 377,000 Mexican-born persons in the United States, while the previous census in 1930 had shown 639,000." As a way ostensibly of dealing with unemployment, officials in California returned several hundred thousand "Mexicans" to Mexico. It is important to note that many of those repatriated were probably actually U.S. citizens by birth, but American officials did not seem overly concerned with such legal niceties (Schaefer, 1993). Nor was economic downturn the only cause of repatriation programs. In earlier periods, deportation was used as a tool for breaking union organizing among Mexican and Mexican-American farm laborers (Helmer, 1975). Further, during World War II when there was a labor shortage in the U.S., the *Braceros* program was set up to bring in needed farm laborers from Mexico (Meier & Ribera, 1993). By the 1950s, though, American officials became concerned with so-called illegal aliens, particularly Mexican, in the U.S., and the Eisenhower administration developed "Operation Wetback," a new deportation program intended to return undocumented Mexican workers to their native country. In 1954 alone, over one million people were caught and deported (Garcia, 1980). Concerns about undocumented or "illegal" aliens, especially in the Southwest, continue to be a major immigration issue in contemporary times.

Puerto Ricans are the second largest group among Hispanics, accounting for 11% of the total in 1996 (del Pinal & Singer, 1997). This island in the Caribbean, which was ceded to the U.S. by Spain as war booty after the Spanish-American War of 1898, holds a unique position as a possession of the United States. According to Melendez and Melendez (1989, p. 3):

> For 92 years Puerto Rico has occupied a peculiar status within the American political system. The United States has never had an established colonial policy and nearly all newly-acquired territories have been incorporated into a process leading to statehood. The island remains an 'unincorporated territory,' belonging to but not being a part, of the United States. Yet Puerto Ricans, as people, have been American citizens since 1917.

Since Puerto Ricans are U.S. citizens, they can freely move between the island and the mainland, with about half of the total population residing in each area (del Pinal & Singer, 1997). While immigration policies do not apply, those especially who come to the mainland find themselves the objects of discrimination and prejudice (Marger, 1991). Furthermore, it is only on the mainland that Puerto Ricans are counted as part of the Hispanic population, since Puerto Rico collects its own population statistics (del Pinal & Singer, 1997). The nearly four million residents of Puerto Rico, then, are not included in the official Census Bureau count of Hispanics.

In 1996, the 1,127,000 Cubans in the U.S. accounted for about 4% of the Hispanic population (del Pinal & Singer, 1997). This group also reflects a unique position in the U.S. Prior to Castro's assumption of power in Cuba in 1959, there was very little Cuban immigration to the U.S. Most immigration, then, has been during the past four decades. Furthermore, political factors have strongly influenced this immigration: "Cuba has been the major source of political refugees from this hemisphere, contributing more than 92% of the 597,000 refugees and asylees from the Americas who were granted permanent residency status between 1946 and 1995" (del Pinal & Singer, 1997, p. 24). U.S. opposition to Castro has led to unique immigration opportunities for Cubans, relative to other immigration from the Caribbean and Central and South America. Circumstances have changed in the recent past, though, with growing opposition to the large numbers of *balseros,* refugees attempting to make the ninety-mile journey on makeshift boats and rafts. Efforts are now made by the U.S. Coast Guard to intercept such refugees and to return them to Cuba.

Recent Immigration Laws

Increasing numbers of immigrants are coming from the Caribbean and from Central and South America, but these individuals are subject to U.S. immigration policies, including quotas and refugee status. Much of this migration has been prompted by U.S. military and political intervention, economic disruptions, international trade arrangements such as the North American Free Trade Agreement, and natural disasters. There have been major changes in immigration policy during the past twenty years, such as the Refugee Act of 1980, which broadened the definition of political refugee by adopting UN definitions. However, because of limits on the numbers of people who are allowed to enter legally, there has been increasing concern with undocumented immigrants; i.e., with so-called "illegal aliens."

One of the most significant policy changes was the Immigration Reform and Control Act of 1986. In order to reduce illegal immigration, proponents of this legislation proposed two methods for resolving the problem: (1) granting amnesty to current undocumented immigrants living in the U.S. and (2) imposing sanctions on employers who hired illegals in the future. Nearly 2,700,000 people were granted amnesty and became legal residents. However, the employer sanctions did not work as intended, partly because the INS was unable to implement effective enforcement procedures and partly because undocumented workers were able to obtain false documents (Martin & Midgley, 1999). Economic problems throughout Latin America have continued to fuel immigration to the U.S., and the illegal population was estimated at 5,275,000 people in 1997 (Martin & Midgley, 1999).

The Illegal Immigration Reform and Immigrant Responsibility Act of 1996, the most recent attempt to further reduce illegal immigration, contained additional and even more punitive provisions than the 1986 legislation. It increased the number of border patrol agents, established a program for employers to verify the status of new employees, and required sponsors of new immigrants to have incomes presumably at levels high enough to ensure that immigrants would not need public assistance, as well as requiring sponsors to sign pledges of support, thus restricting access of legal immigrants to human and social services (Martin & Midgley, 1999). Other legislation approved that same year also affected new immigrants, particularly the Personal Responsibility and Work Opportunity Reconciliation Act (which will be discussed later) and the Antiterrorism and Effective Death Penalty Act. In general, recent "reforms" in immigration policy continue to restrict legal entry into the U.S. for many people.

Militarization of the Mexico-U.S. Border

Since at least the 1950s, officials and public figures have increasingly voiced concerns about so-called illegal immigration to the United States. As Nagengast (1998, p. 38) has noted, "Throughout the 1980s and 1990s, opinion makers, politicians, and Congress have portrayed the border area and the communities within it as places 'infested' with hordes of drug runners, welfare cheats and foreigners looking for a free ride." There is now a profound public perception of illegal immigration as a serious social problem, especially on the West Coast, in the Southwest, and in Florida. One rather quiet outgrowth of these perceptions has been an expanding U.S. military presence along the 1,600 mile border separating the U.S. and Mexico.

The Posse Comitatus Act of 1878 banned the use of the military in law enforcement, including patrolling the border. However, the Reagan administration's "war on drugs" began to change that policy, and presidential, congressional, and court actions since the early 1980s have led to a significant militarization of the border. According to Palafox (1996, p. 15), "Exceptions created expressly for antidrug operations cracked open the door; the Clinton administration is opening it wider still in the politically expedient campaign to thwart unwanted immigrants."

Border patrol units started receiving special paramilitary training operations in 1984, about the same time that Congress began to authorize increasing numbers of agents. Then, in 1989, Congress authorized 5,000 soldiers for border patrol duty. More recent efforts to increase the number of troops have been defeated in Congress, but the Border Patrol itself has received special training for over a decade now, and military units have provided long-term assistance by developing advanced helicopter pads and roads along the border, which improved the ability of the Border Patrol to carry out "special," military-style operations (Nagengast, 1998).

While this "militarization" of the border raises serious issues about potential human rights violations (Kaminer, 1999), it has also created an atmosphere where violence toward and callous treatment of its targets is likely to occur. The 1997 killing of Ezequiel Hernandez by U.S. marines, which created a furor at the time, is but one example. Hernandez was a high school sophomore who was herding sheep when he was shot. Yet the marines who shot him were exonerated because he supposedly fit the profile of a drug dealer (Nagengast, 1998). Unfortunately, intensifying efforts to "control" the border have led to increasing deaths, at least 1,200 between 1993 and 1996. Harassment of Latinos throughout the Southwest, whether U.S.-born or immigrant, has proliferated as well (de Uriarte, 1996), and abuses by the Border Patrol continue to rise (Light, 1996).

IMMIGRANTS, WELFARE, AND OFFICIAL LANGUAGE POLICY

Explicit anti-immigrant measures such as those described in the previous overview of U.S. immigration policy are also found in other areas of recent U.S. policy. Two specific areas are social welfare policy and official language policy. Changes in both of these areas reflect growing controversy over immigration, multiculturalism, and public assistance. This controversy is fueled by misperceptions regarding the cost of the immigrant population to the nation, particularly Latino immigrants, in the areas of social welfare and bilingual programs (the U.S. English organization refers to the latter as "linguistic welfare"). In this section, we will provide a brief overview of research regarding the cost and contribution of immigrants to the U.S., and describe the recent changes in social and "linguistic welfare" programming.

The Cost and Contribution of Immigrants

Both immigration and welfare are hotly debated issues in the United States, and their intersection is even more controversial. Not surprisingly, given the emotionally and politically charged nature of these two issues, the national debate is riddled with misperceptions, misrepresentations, and misunderstandings. Some of the popular misperceptions include a belief (1) that most or a large proportion of immigrants to the U.S. come here illegally; (2) that public benefit programs are generally available to and widely used by immigrants, and (3) that the "generous" U.S. social welfare system serves as a magnet attracting immigrants.

A closer look presents a different picture. First, roughly 800,000 immigrants/refugees enter this country legally on an annual basis: 675,000 immigrants come as legal permanent residents and another 120,000 are admitted as refugees. In contrast, it is estimated that roughly 300,000, a much smaller number, enter the country as undocumented immigrants. Secondly, most immigrants, including those most recently arriving, are restricted from receiving most forms of welfare or public assistance. Most legal immigrants are barred from receiving benefits from welfare programs for five years after their arrival, and undocumented immigrants are permanently denied all major social services except for emergency medical services (Impoco, 1994). Nevertheless, the popular belief that immigrants (both legal and illegal) are heavy welfare users persists and is fueled by research that paints an incomplete or inaccurate picture of the situation (Fix & Passel, 1994).

There is also the misperception that certain groups of immigrants, primarily Latinos, are much more likely to end up on welfare than others. The truth is that refugees and elderly newcomers are most likely to receive public benefits and the sending countries of these immigrants are generally not Latin American, with the exception of Cuba. A recent analysis (prior to 1996 welfare changes) of the proportion of immigrants, in rank order, receiving welfare by place of birth demonstrates this: Cambodia (28%), Laos (27%), former Soviet Union (20%), Vietnam (16%), Cuba (10%), Dominican Republic (9%), China (6%), Philippines (4%), South Korea (4%), and Mexico (2%) (Impoco, 1994, p. 38). Note that immigrants from countries with the largest proportion of welfare recipients are those that the U.S. government has designated for consideration for refugee status.

In an analysis of recent research focusing on the impact of immigrants on the public sector, Fix and Passel (1994) conclude that studies conducted by government agencies who have an interest in recovering the costs of immigrants or non-profit groups committed to reducing immigration levels in the U.S. have dominated the literature. While they note the varying conclusions and quality of the research, Fix and Passel argue that the studies all overstate the negative public-sector impact of immigrants by (1) understating tax collection from immigrants; (2) overstating service costs of immigrants; (3) ignoring the economic benefits of immigrant consumer spending and immigrant-owned businesses; (4) overstating job displacement impacts and costs; (5) omitting parallel analysis for the native-born which would provide a reference for comparison that would indicate that the native-born are also net tax users; and (6) overstating the size of the immigrant population, particularly the undocumented immigrant population.

Fix and Passel (1994) conclude that welfare use among immigrants is slightly higher than that of the native-born population, but that when social and economic characteristics are held constant, immigrant households are no more likely to receive welfare than are native households. On average about 4.2% of the U.S. native-born population reports receiving welfare compared to 4.7% of immigrants. Among the non-refugee immigrant working age immigrant population, welfare use falls below that of the working age native-born, 2.7% and 3.7% respectively.

Personal Responsibility and Work Opportunity Reconciliation Act of 1996

In 1996, Congress enacted the Personal Responsibility and Work Opportunity Reconciliation Act (PRWORA) in order "to end welfare as we know it." Among the numerous changes mandated by the Act, several significant changes targeted immigrant recipients. The Act makes several statements regarding immigration and welfare, including (1) self-sufficiency as the basic principle in immigration law; (2) that aliens within U.S. borders should not depend on the government but rather on their own capabilities and sponsor families; (3) that public benefits should not constitute an incentive for immigration; and (4) that current provisions have proven to be unsuccessful in insuring that individual aliens do not burden the public benefit system (Cristol-Deman & Edwards, 1998).

The Act denies Supplemental Security Income (SSI) benefits and Food Stamps to immigrants, including legal immigrants who have resided in the U.S. for years, unless they qualify for an exemption.

These changes are far reaching, with the U.S. budget office estimating that as many as 500,00 legal immigrants will be affected by the policy change. There are four major categories of exemptions: (1) refugees or asylees; (2) those granted a withholding of deportation by the INS; (3) immigrant U.S. military personnel and their dependents; and (4) working non-U.S. citizens who have legally been employed in the U.S. for more than 40 "qualifying quarters" (ten years) and their dependent children. However, qualifying immigrants are also subject to the general provisions of the Act that include a five-year lifetime limit on welfare benefits (Stubbs, 1997).

The Act also contains a five-year prospective ban on all federal benefits means-tested programs to qualified immigrants who entered the U.S. after August 26, 1996. Before passage of the Act, qualified legal immigrants were eligible for welfare and other benefits immediately upon gaining legal status.

The Congressional Budget Office has estimated that the total savings resulting from these welfare changes will be roughly $54 billion in the six-year period following passage of the Act. Of that total, between $20 and 25 billion (or roughly 45% of the savings) will come from changes targeting immigrants (Cristol-Deman & Edwards, 1998).

Also under the Act, states are given broader power to determine eligibility of "qualified" immigrants for state-funded programs. Before the Act, states could not discriminate against legal immigrants in the provision of benefits, but now states can choose to deny, limit, or extend access to locally funded aid such as general assistance. States also retain the option to deny non-emergency Medicaid, social services block grants, and the Supplemental Food Program for Women Infants and Children (WIC). There is tremendous variation among states. For example, New York continues to provide public assistance benefits to women and children regardless of their immigration status, while California has chosen to drop "unqualified immigrants" (Stubbs, 1997).

Since the PRWORA became law in 1996, there have been several partial restorations of benefits to immigrants. The Balanced Budget Act of 1997 restored SSI and Medicaid benefits to pre-PRWORA eligible qualified immigrants who were terminated. It also provides for SSI and Medicaid benefits for immigrants in the country as of August 22, 1996 who were not receiving benefits at that time, but who subsequently become disabled. In June 1998, Clinton signed the Agricultural Research Act into Law. This Act restored food stamp benefits to pre-PRWORA qualified immigrant children, persons receiving disability related assistance, and seniors. The Agricultural Research Act also restored benefits to Hmong immigrants (Clinton & Gore, 1999).

Linguistic Welfare and the English-Only Movement

The imposition of English was part of a larger aggressive program of Americanization in the early 1900s. Several laws were passed during this period requiring English for civic and political participation. The ability to speak English was made a condition for citizenship in 1906, and nine years later an English-literacy requirement was added. Several other examples from this era included an Oregon statute that required the English translation of the entire content of all foreign language periodicals, a Nebraska statute that ordered that all public meetings be conducted in English, and the passage of laws restricting or prohibiting foreign language instruction in primary schools (Nunberg, 1997).

Recent polls indicate significant support for making English the official language of the U.S., reporting between 65% and 86% favoring such a policy. The underlying assumptions of many official language policy supporters are (1) that recent immigrants, particularly those from Latin America, in contrast to earlier immigrants, do not learn nor desire to learn English, and (2) that this refusal to learn English costs the nation in terms of bilingual or Spanish programming, as well as threatening the nation's identity and social institutions. The late Senator S. I. Hayakawa (R-Calif), summarized this position in the following statement: "Large populations of Mexican Americans, Cubans, and Puerto Ricans do not speak English and have no intention of learning . . . For the first time in our history, our nation is faced with the possibility of the kind of linguistic division that has torn apart Canada in recent years; that has been a major feature of the unhappy Belgium, split into the French and Flemish; that is at the very moment a bloody division between the Sinhalese and Tamil populations of Sri Lanka" (cited in Nunberg, 1997, pp. 42-43).

Like social welfare, the public debate regarding immigrants and English language use are filled with misperceptions. Contrary to popular beliefs, most immigrants want to learn English and do so relatively quickly. For example, more than 90% of first-generation California-born Latinos have native fluency in English, according to a recent Rand study, and demographer Calvin Veltman has noted that the traditional three-generation period for a complete language shift has been shortened to one among recent immigrants (Nunberg, 1997). Older immigrants wait on long lists for ESL class openings nearly everywhere in the U.S. (Reimers, 1998)

The late Senator Hayakawa first introduced his English Language Amendment (ELA) to the U.S. Constitution in 1981. The purpose of ELA was to establish English as the official language of the nation. While Hayakawa's proposal never made it out of committee, it has resurfaced in different forms several times since. In 1994, following the Republican congressional victory, Wisconsin Republican Representative Toby Roth reintroduced his version, the Declaration of Official Language Act. During his presidential bid in the last election, Bob Dole reintroduced official English into the national agenda when he endorsed the English Language Amendment. In contrast, President Clinton and Vice President and current presidential candidate Al Gore (1999) have recently stated that they have strongly opposed legislation to make English the official language of the U.S. since that would have jeopardized assistance to tens of thousands of new immigrants and others seeking to learn English as adults.

While the efforts of English-only proponents have not been very successful at the national level, they have been quite successful at the state level. Popular support for English as the official language has been advanced aggressively by organizations such as U.S. English and English First, established in 1983 and 1986 respectively, with Senator Hayakawa as the first head of U.S. English. By 1996, U.S. English reported a membership of over 600,000, and 23 states had adopted official-language measures through either referenda or legislative action (Reimers, 1998).

However, the nature of state laws varies, with some states passing largely symbolic acts such as that of Arkansas (signed by Clinton when he was Governor in 1987 but which he has since noted was "a mistake"), which simply states: "The English language shall be the official language of the state of Arkansas." Other states have passed more repressive laws such as Arizona's 1988 voter supported law that prohibits the state or its employees from conducting business in any language other than English, with the limited exception of health and public safety emergencies. Furthermore, English-only policies are not limited to the public sector. In recent years, numerous private firms and institutions have adopted English-only workplace policies. These policies prohibit the use of a foreign language by employees when interacting with the public and even when speaking with coworkers or when on breaks (Nunberg, 1997).

While much of the focus of official language legislation supporters has been on eliminating bilingual ballots, foreign language drivers' license examinations, and the use of foreign languages by federal programs to reach into ethnic communities, many of these individuals also reject bilingual education programs, arguing, "Bilingual education has resegregated the schools along language lines, and isolated immigrant youngsters from their American peers; it has eroded teaching standards through 'emergency' certification of unqualified teachers; it has entrenched the federal role in running local schools; and it has politicized our schools as no issue has ever before" (U.S. Senate, 1984, cited in Hobson et al. 1998, p. 149). Yet it is important to note that some critics of bilingual education have come from individuals who reject official language legislation. One such detractor, historian Arthur Schlesinger, has noted that "bilingualism has not worked out as planned; rather the contrary . . . Bilingual education retards rather than expedites the movement of Hispanic children into the English-speaking world and promotes segregation more than it does integration" (cited in Reimers, 1998, p. 126).

Like official language policies, bilingual education has a long history in the United States. Bilingual programming in public schools, primarily German and Spanish, was common in the late nineteenth and early twentieth centuries, but was largely eliminated in the World War I era of anti-foreign madness. The contemporary system of bilingual education was initiated in the 1960s in response to large numbers of Cubans arriving in Miami following the Cuban revolution. This initial program was quite successful, and other communities began modified versions of the Miami model. However, federal support for bilingual programs, with the exception of the Cuban refugee targeted program, did not receive federal support until the passage of the 1968 Bilingual Education Act. In 1974 federal programs and funding were expanded significantly to include teacher training and aid for schools (Reimers, 1998).

The expansion of federal support for bilingual education did not happen without controversy. Controversy grew after the election in

1980 of Ronald Reagan, who led an attack on bilingual education. While bilingual education survived this assault, federal guidelines were modified and funds trimmed (Reimers, 1998).

Currently, these programs are at the center of several state anti-bilingual education initiatives. In the June 1998 California primary elections, 61% of voters supported Proposition 227. This ballot measure was sponsored by Ron Unz, a Silicon Valley millionaire and board member of the conservative Center for Educational Opportunity (CEO) in Washington, D.C., which "has stated in court papers that it is their business, through referendums, through litigation, and through legislation, to get rid of native language instruction" (Rethinking Schools, 1999, p. 20). The passage of Proposition 227 was a strong victory for anti-bilingual education proponents because it "virtually eliminates bilingual education in California," the nation's leader in limited English proficient students, 25% (roughly 1.3 million students) compared with 6.7% of students nationally (Streisand, 1997, p. 36). The Act requires that all California students in public schools be taught primarily in English unless their parents request otherwise and that limited English proficient pupils be placed in Structured English Immersion (SEI) classes for no more than a year under normal circumstances (California Association of Bilingual Education, 1999).

The efforts of Unz and CEO are not limited to California. Unz is presently assisting in an Arizona effort to launch a similar measure, which is expected to be on the state ballot there in November 2000. He has also announced his intention to place a similar initiative on the Massachusetts ballot in the same time frame (Rethinking Schools, 1999). Unfortunately, attacks on bilingual education are mounting, while indicators of Latino educational achievement demand urgent attention. For example, the 1994 Latino high school dropout rate was 30%, four times that of Anglos (7.7%) (NCLR 1998), and California has a 40% Latino dropout rate (Streisand, 1997). Furthermore, in 1996, 61% of 25 to 29 year old Latinos had completed high school compared to 92.6% of same age whites (NCLR 1998), and, among 15 to 17 year olds, 39.9% of Latinos were retained in grade, in contrast to 29.6% of white students (NCLR 1998).

CONCLUSIONS

Public policy has profoundly shaped the Latino experience in the United States, just as it has the experience of other racial and ethnic minorities. Since the founding of this country, racial and ethnic status has been a critical factor in determining social and political status. For many Hispanics, there was little choice in becoming residents of the U.S., since where they lived was absorbed into the country's boundaries by colonial expansion. Even when they were "guaranteed" rights of citizenship, those laws, such as the Treaty of Guadalupe Hidalgo, were ignored or superseded by local, state, and federal courts and legislative bodies. Latinos were tolerated as residents, but their political and legal rights were often trampled or denied. Even U.S. citizens by birth could (and still do) find themselves treated as aliens and deported to presumed countries of origin, especially Mexico. What better proof is there of a group's position in the social hierarchy than having one's citizenship denied–or simply ignored? Living within certain geographic borders does not mean that a particular social group is accepted by the dominant group as a legitimate part of that community.

Contemporary debates on immigration and public welfare policy are framed by past ideas about American identity; i.e., who should be here and what is the nature of this society. Fears about immigrants as a threat to "our way of life" have been expressed since the birth of the country (Reimers, 1998). While Martin and Midgley (1999) portray the first century of U.S. immigration policy as relatively benign, race and ethnicity, in fact, have been part of the fabric of American immigration law since the Naturalization Act of 1790 (Parrillo, 2000; Takagi, 1989). Race and ethnicity became more blatant in the period that Martin and Midgley characterized as the era of "qualitative restrictions," but they were a major factor in previous images of who should be and who should not be part of the American fabric.

The exclusionary sentiments that were popular at the end of the nineteenth and beginning of the twentieth century revolved around skin color (Takagi, 1989). Social Darwinists had succeeded in establishing a hierarchy of "races," in identifying the "white" race as superior, both intellectually and physically, and the concept of eugenicism grew increasingly popular among both scientists and the educated public toward the end of the nineteenth century (Segal & Kilty, 1998). While the atrocities of the Nazis and other racists of the twentieth century would throw those ideas into disrepute, many such misconceptions and misrepresentations not only survived but have resurfaced in the guise of new ideas (Kilty & Segal, 1996; Kilty & Swank, 1997). Modern day racists such as Arthur Jensen and the late Richard

Herrnstein have kept alive ideas about racial superiority and inferiority (e.g., Herrnstein & Murray, 1994). As we showed earlier, many ideas about Hispanics are misperceptions, misrepresentations, and misunderstandings, but they draw on a legacy of cultural perceptions and beliefs (Rodgriguez, 1997).

The question becomes: who benefits and why? As Lenski (1966, p. 3) so eloquently pointed out in his classic study of social stratification, that is the issue "which underlies all the discussions of classes and strata and their structural relationships." Social structure provides a mechanism for distribution of the valued resources, including wealth, status, privilege, etc., in a given society, and racial and ethnic categories are a part of that distributive structure. Racial and ethnic position separate the "haves" from the "have nots," just as does social class. Virtually every non-white group in the U.S. is and has been economically and socially disadvantaged compared to the dominant white or Anglo group (Feagin & Feagin, 1999). Throughout the nineteenth and twentieth centuries, some social scientists and other authorities have attempted to justify those differences by arguing that certain groups are "innately superior" and others "innately inferior." From the Social Darwinists of the 1800s to the scientific racists of the late twentieth century who point to genes as the mechanism underlying presumed group differences, these ideas have endured in our culture (Kilty & Segal, 1996).

Why are public policy debates about immigration, social welfare, and the Hispanic community fueled by distortions and misperceptions? These ideas, most simply old ones recast as something new, reflect ideological positions and the agenda of powerful interests. The media restate old ideas as new because of commanding stakeholders which own and control them. Political figures present old ideas about immigration and exclusion as though new because those political figures are supported by the people at the top; i.e., those who own and control the major industries and corporations that make up the American economic structure, including the media (McChesney, 1999). Conservative think-tanks and foundations present old information in the guise of something new and have come to dominate the attention of media figures because they represent and are funded by those at the top who own the media which disseminates these ideas and beliefs (Stefancic & Delgado, 1996). Those at the top of the social structure have an obvious vested interest in maintaining their domination and control, and they have the means for setting the social and public agenda.

Long ago, those at the top learned a simple but powerful strategy for controlling the masses: divide and conquer. In the early days of America, the colonial masters used this device to separate white from black and red, to eliminate white resistance and to break down a united front among the working class even when the mass of white people were being exploited by the ruling elite (Bennett, 1975). Nativism, racism, and exclusion have long been used to divide and separate those at the bottom of the U.S. social hierarchy. Portraying Latinos as coming to the U.S. illegally in large numbers, as attracted by "generous" public assistance programs, and as more likely to "take advantage" of public welfare paints a negative picture of Latinos that is consistent with past images. Focusing on Latin American roots has also led to a "racialization" process (i.e., a racial group formation process) that helps to identify Latinos as "outsiders," especially since most are readily discernible to Anglos in skin color (Marger, 1991). Unfortunately, because of the long legacy of the strategy of divide and conquer, other racial and ethnic groups, particularly Blacks, who are also in disadvantaged circumstances may see Hispanics as competitors rather than as potential allies against the dominant group (Rodriguez, 1996).

It is essential for Latinos to resist how they are depicted and to present as widely as possible the reality of the Hispanic experience and condition in this society. As their numbers grow, so do their resources and ability to present alternative ideas. In addition, it is imperative for Hispanics to break through this "divide and conquer" strategy of the elite and to develop coalitions with other racial and ethnic groups. Most other non-white groups also experience depictions of their positions that are misleading. By combining resources, such coalitions are more likely to impact on the perceptions, beliefs, and understandings of the majority population, especially in this conservative political and social era.

REFERENCES

Bennett, L., Jr. (1975). The road not taken. In L. Bennett, Jr., *The Shaping of Black America* (pp. 61-80). New York: Penguin.

California Association of Bilingual Education. (1999). Implementing proposition 227: Answers to commonly-asked questions. http://www.bilingualeducation.org/current.htm.

Clinton, W. J. & Gore, A. (1999). Working on behalf of the Hispanic community. Press Release, The White House, Washington, DC.

Cristol-Deman, L. & Edwards, R. (1998). Closing the door on the immigrant poor. *Stanford Law and Policy Review,* 9 (1), 141-163.

Day, J. C. (1996). *Population projections of the United States by age, sex, race, and Hispanic origin: 1995 to 2050.* (U.S. Bureau of the Census, Current Population Reports, P25-1130). Washington, DC 1996.

de Uriarte, M. L. (1996). Baiting immigrants: Heartbreak for Latinos. *The Progressive,* 60 (September), 18-20.

del Castillo, R. G. (1996). The Treaty of Guadalupe Hidalgo. In O. J. Martinez (Ed.), *U.S.-Mexico borderlands: Historical and contemporary perspectives* (pp. 2-9). Wilmington, DE: SR Books.

del Pinal, J., & Singer, A. (1997). Generations of diversity: Latinos in the United States. *Population Bulletin,* 52 (October), 1-48.

Drinnon, R. (1990). *Facing west: The metaphysics of Indian hating and empire building.* New York: Schocken.

Feagin, J. R., & Feagin, C. B. (1999). *Racial and ethnic relations.* (6th ed.) Englewood Cliffs, NJ: Prentice Hall.

Fix, M. E., & Passel, J. S. (1994). Setting the record straight: What are the costs to the public? *Public Welfare,* 53 (2), 6-10.

Garcia, J. R. (1980). *Operation wetback: The mass deportation of Mexican undocumented workers in 1954.* Westport, CT: Greenwood.

Gibson, C., & Lennon, E. (1999). *Historical census statistics on the foreign-born population of the United States: 1850 to 1990.* (Population Division Working Paper No. 29). Washington, DC: Population Division, U.S. Bureau of the Census.

Gonzalez, R. (1998). National Council of La Raza 1998 annual conference focuses on Latino education. *Agenda,* 14 (2), 8-9.

Helmer, J. (1975). *Drugs and minority oppression.* New York: Seabury.

Herrnstein, R. J., & Murray, C. (1994). *The bell curve: Intelligence and class structure in American life.* New York: Free Press.

Hopson, R. K., Green, P. E., Yeakeay, C. C., Richardson, J. W., & Reed, Tracey A. (1988). Language and social policy: An analysis of forces that drive official language politics in the United States. *Chicago Policy Review,* 22 (Spring), 1-24.

Hraba, J. (1994). *American ethnicity.* (2nd. ed.) Itasca, IL: Peacock.

Impoco, J. (1994). Shutting the golden door: Economic fear, ethnic prejudice and politics as usual make the melting pot a pressure cooker. *U.S. News and World Report,* October 3, 36-40.

Kaminer, W. (1999). Taking liberties: The new assault on freedom. *American Prospect,* 35 (January-February), 33-40.

Kilty, K. M., & Segal, E. A. (1996). Genetics and biological determinism: Scientific breakthrough or blaming the victim revisited? *Humanity and Society,* 20, 90-110.

Kilty, K. M., & Swank, E. (1997). Institutional racism and media representations: Depictions of violent criminals and welfare recipients. *Sociological Imagination,* 34, 105-128.

Lenski, G. E. (1966). *Power and privilege: A theory of social stratification.* New York: McGraw-Hill.

Light, J. (1996). Baiting immigrants: Women bear the brunt. *The Progressive,* 60 (September), 21-23.

Marger, M. N. (1991). *Race and ethnic relations: American and Global Perspectives.* (2nd ed.) Belmont, CA: Wadsworth.

Martin, P., & Midgley, E. (1994). Immigration to the United States: Journey to an uncertain destination. *Population Bulletin,* 49 (September), 1-47.

Martin, P., & Midgley, E. (1999). Immigration to the United States. *Population Bulletin,* 54 (June), 1-44.

Martinez, O. J. (1996). The making of the boundary. In O. J. Martinez (ed.), *U.S.-Mexico borderlands: Historical and contemporary perspectives* (p. 1). Wilmington, DE: SR Books.

McChesney, R. W. (1999). *Rich media, poor democracy: Communication politics in dubious times.* Champaign, IL: University of Illinois Press.

Meier, M. S., & Ribera, F. (1993). *Mexican Americans/American Mexicans.* New York: Hill and Wang.

Melendez, E., & Melendez, E. (1989). Introduction: Puerto Rico: A colonial dilemma. *Radical America,* 23 (January-February), 3-7.

Nagengast, C. (1998). Militarizing the border patrol. *NACLA Report on the Americas,* XXXII (No. 3), 37-41.

Northrup, D. (1995). *Indentured labor in the age of imperialism, 1834-1922.* New York: Cambridge University Press.

Nunberg, G. (1997). Lingo jingo: English only and the new nativism. *The American Prospect,* 33 (July-August), 40-48.

Palafox, J. (1996). Militarizing the border. *CovertAction Quarterly,* Number 56 (Spring), 14-19.

Parrillo, V. N. (2000). *Strangers to these shores.* (6th ed.) Boston: Allyn & Bacon.

Portes, A., & Rumbaut, R. G. (1996). *Immigrant America: A portrait.* (2nd. ed.) Berkeley, CA: University of California Press.

Reimers, D. M. (1998). *Unwelcome strangers: American identity and the turn against immigration.* New York: Columbia University Press.

Rethinking Schools. (1999). Coming soon: The son of Unz. *Rethinking Schools: An Urban Education Journal,* 13 (Summer), 20.

Rodriguez, C. E. (Ed.) (1997). *Latin looks: Images and Latinas and Latinos in the U. S. media.* Boulder, CO: Westview.

Rodriguez, N. (1996). U.S. immigration and intergroup relations: African Americans and Latinos. *Social Justice,* 23 (3), 111-124.

Schaefer, R. T. (1993). *Racial and ethnic groups.* New York: HarperCollins.

Segal, E. A., & Kilty, K. M. (1998). The resurgence of biological determinism and the assault on human diversity. *Race, Gender & Class,* 5, 61-75.

Stefancic, J., & Delgado, R. (1996). *No mercy: How conservative think tanks and foundations changed America's social agenda.* Philadelphia: Temple University Press.

Streisand, B. (1997). Is it hasta la vista for bilingual ed. *U. S. News & World Report,* November 24, 36-38.

Stubbs, E. (1997). Welfare and immigration reform: Refusing aid to immigrants. *Berkeley Women's Law Journal,* 12, 151-157.

Takagi, R. (1989). *Strangers from a different shore: A history of Asian Americans.* New York: Penguin.

An Analysis of Latino Poverty and a Plan of Action

Mario R. De La Rosa

SUMMARY. This paper provides a broad overview of the current poverty status of Latinos in the United States. Data from the 1996 U.S. Census indicates that poverty affects Latinos disproportionately and that Latinos' low educational attainment and poor occupational status participation have a great impact on the current poverty conditions of Latinos. Also discussed are the effects of poverty on the well-being of Latinos. The findings from the U.S. Census and several major health surveys suggest that there is a relationship between poverty and Latino current health and educational status. Recommendations are made by the author to alleviate the conditions of poverty faced by Latinos. *[Article copies available for a fee from The Haworth Document Delivery Service: 1-800-342-9678. E-mail address: <getinfo@haworthpressinc.com> Website: <http://www.haworthpressinc.com>]*

KEYWORDS. Poverty, Latinos, causes, consequences

INTRODUCTION

According to many Latino leaders, poverty is the most serious social problem faced by Latinos nationwide (National Council of La

Mario R. De La Rosa, PhD, is Associate Professor at the School of Social Work at Florida International University.

Address all correspondence to: Dr. Mario De La Rosa, School of Social Work, Florida International University, AC 1, #245, 3000 Northeast 145th St., Miami, FL 33181.

[Haworth co-indexing entry note]: "An Analysis of Latino Poverty and a Plan of Action." De La Rosa, Mario R. Co-published simultaneously in *Journal of Poverty* (The Haworth Press, Inc.) Vol. 4, No. 1/2, 2000, pp. 27-62; and: *Latino Poverty in the New Century: Inequalities, Challenges and Barriers* (ed: Maria Vidal de Haymes, Keith M. Kilty, and Elizabeth A. Segal) The Haworth Press, Inc., 2000, pp. 27-62. Single or multiple copies of this article are available for a fee from The Haworth Document Delivery Service [1-800-342-9678, 9:00 a.m. - 5:00 p.m. (EST). E-mail address: getinfo@haworthpressinc.com].

Raza, 1990). Many of these Latino leaders believe that if the impoverished conditions of Latinos are not effectively addressed, their economic and social position in American society will worsen. This grim assessment by Latino leaders comes at a time in our country's history when Latinos are expected to become the largest minority group in this country (U.S. Department Bureau of the Census, 1997a). It also comes at a time when Latinos are beginning to influence the American political landscape (Purdum, 1998). In spite of the Latino leadership's concerns with the plight of poor Latinos, few social and economic policies and programs have been developed and implemented by the U.S. government to address the growing problem of poverty among Latinos. While political and economic forces are mostly responsible for this inaction, many Latino leaders are convinced that the lack of knowledge about the causes and consequences of poverty among Latinos has exacerbated government inactions in addressing the plight of poor Latinos (Aponte, 1993).

A review of the literature on this topic by this paper's author confirms Latino leaders' concerns. Few studies exist which provide a broad understanding of the factors responsible for poverty among Latinos and its devastating consequences on their well-being. The lack of understanding of Latino poverty comes in spite of the wealth of information available from the U.S. Census and other data sources on the poverty conditions of Latinos (see Aponte, 1993; Perez & De la Rosa, 1993, *The Journal of the American Medical Association* (JAMA), 1991).

Purpose

Therefore, the intent of this paper is to begin to fill the void in knowledge which many Latino leaders believe is partly responsible for the lack of action by policy makers at the federal and state governmental levels in addressing the serious problem of poverty confronting Latinos. This paper will provide a framework for understanding this problem in the United States as well as for identifying the steps that need to be taken to remedy it. This paper, then, will discuss the extent, cause and consequences of poverty among Latinos, and possible solutions. To accomplish this objective, this paper is divided into five major sections: (1) an overview of the poverty condition of Latinos in the United States; (2) the causes of poverty among Latinos; (3) the consequences of poverty; (4) recommendations for reducing poverty among Latinos; and (5) strategies for implementing the recommendations.

Before proceeding with the text of this paper, several remarks need to be made about its purpose and the limitations of the data presented. This paper is not intended to provide an exhaustive overview of the problem of poverty among Latinos. This paper is merely intended to provide a framework for discussing issues and concerns associated with the problem of Latino poverty. Its recommendations are also not exhaustive and are only meant to generate further discussion on the topic. Many of the issues, concerns, and recommendations presented in this paper warrant separate chapters.

Furthermore, there are several limitations regarding the data presented in this paper. One, the author will rely primarily on data from the U.S. Census Bureau of Labor Statistics, and several national health surveys. Many important state and local surveys and epidemiologic studies providing important information regarding the conditions of Latino impoverishment have not been included. Two, most of the data reported in this paper refers to Latinos as a homogenous group without taking into account national origin or within- or between-group differences among the major Latino subgroups (i.e., Cuban-Americans, Mexican-Americans, Puerto Ricans, and South and Central Americans). Therefore, the conclusions reached from the data reported cannot be used to generalize about the poverty conditions, or their causes or consequences for specific Latino subgroups. However, whenever possible, efforts will be made to report data that provides information about within-group as well as between-group differences among the four Latino subgroups.

POVERTY CONDITIONS OF LATINOS: HOW SERIOUS IS THE PROBLEM?

Recent data from the U.S. Census indicates that poverty affects Latinos disproportionately (U.S. Department of Commerce, Bureau of the Census, 1997b). The findings from the U.S. Census, as shown in Table 1, reveal that about one-third of the more than 29 million Latinos living in the United States in 1996 were living in poverty compared to 11.2% of white non-Latino persons. It should be noted that the U.S. Census data excludes Puerto Ricans living on the island of Puerto Rico from this survey. Data from the 1996 U.S. Census, as

TABLE 1. 1996 Poverty Rates for Persons and Families by Race/Ethnicity and Selected Characteristics

All Persons	Black	Latino	White
Both Sexes	28.4	29.4	11.2
Under 18 Years	39.9	40.3	16.3
65 Years and Over	25.3	24.4	9.4
Families	**Black**	**Latino**	**White**
Married Families	10.6	21.5	10.6
Single Female Head-of-Household	52.8	61.2	35.9
Single Female Head-of-Household under 18 Years	58.2	67.5	43.2

Source: U.S. Department of Commerce, Bureau of the Census, 1997b.

shown in Table 1, also shows that poverty is a very serious problem among Latino children and adolescents. Among Latinos age 18 and younger, 40.3% were living in poverty compared to 16.3% of white non-Latino children and adolescents age 18 and younger. Poverty is also a serious problem among the Latino elderly. Although data from the 1996 U.S. Census indicates that Latino elderly poverty rates were lower than those for Latino youth, the poverty rates of Latino elderly 65 years and older were almost three times higher than those of their white non-Latino counterparts.

Data from the 1996 U.S. Census also makes it clear that many Latino families live in poverty. The poverty rates for Latino families, as shown in Table 1, were much higher than the poverty rates for black and white non-Latino families (U.S. Department of Commerce, Bureau of the Census, 1997b). In particular, the poverty rates of Latino families headed by single females were astoundingly high. Sixty-one percent of such families were described as impoverished in contrast to 52.8% percent of black families, and 38.9% of white non-Latino families. Among single female heads-of-household age 18 and younger, the rates were even higher for Latino than black, or white non-Latino families (see Table 1). Among married Latino families, however, the poverty rates were much lower than among families headed by a single female. Nevertheless, the poverty rate for Latino married families was still more than three times the rate of white non-Latino married families (see Table 1). In addition, trend data available from the U.S. Census also indicates that the conditions of poverty of Latinos have not changed much during the past fifteen years. U.S. Census statistics reveal that the poverty rates for Latino persons and families during the 1980s and early 1990s are similar to the poverty rates reported on Latinos by the 1996 U.S. Census (U.S. Department of Commerce, Bureau of the Census, 1996).

The 1996 U.S. Census data also suggests that a high percentage of persons and families of Mexican-American and Puerto Rican ancestry were living in poverty (U.S. Department of Commerce, Bureau of the Census, 1997c). These two Latino subgroups comprise 73.7% of the total U.S. Latino population (Mexican-Americans, 63.2% and Puerto Ricans, 10.5%). Unfortunately, data is not readily available from the U.S. Census on the poverty rates for persons and families of Cuban or South and Central American ancestry. The lack of data does not allow researchers to determine whether the poverty rates for persons and families of South and Central American and Cuban ancestries are higher or lower than those of persons and families of Mexican-American and Puerto Rican ancestry.

The 1996 U.S. Census, as shown in Table 2, also reports that, except

TABLE 2. 1996 Poverty Rates for Mexican-American and Puerto Rican Persons and Families by Selected Characteristics (Percentages)

All Persons	Mexican-Americans	Puerto Ricans
Both Sexes	31.0	35.7
Under 18 Years	41.0	49.9
65 Years and Over	25.1	27.3
Families		
Married Families	25.2	14.6
Single Female Head-of-Household	55.4	64.8
Single Female Head-of-Household Under 18 Years	68.1	76.6

Source: U.S. Department of Commerce, Bureau of the Census, 1997c.

for married families, Puerto Ricans had higher poverty rates than Mexican-Americans and Latinos as an aggregate group (U.S. Department of Commerce, Bureau of the Census, 1997c). Particularly striking are the poverty rates of Puerto Rican single female heads-of-household. More than 64% of Puerto Rican single female heads-of-household lived in poverty compared to 54.4% of Mexican-Americans and 61.5% of all Latinos (see Table 2). On the other hand, the 1996 U.S. Census shows that Puerto Rican married families had significantly lower poverty rates than Mexican-American married couples. As shown in Table 2, Puerto Rican married couples had a poverty rate twice as low as that of Mexican-American married couples. In addition, the poverty rates of Puerto Rican married families were also much lower than those of all Latino married families (see Table 1). Furthermore, trend data available from the U.S. Census makes clear that during the 1980s and early 1990s, with the exception of married families, the poverty rates for Puerto Rican persons and families were higher than those for Mexican-American persons and families (U.S. Department of Commerce, Bureau of the Census, 1997c).

Notwithstanding the weaknesses in the poverty measurements used by the U.S. Census (see National Research Council, 1996; Brooks-Gunn et al., 1995), these data provide a broad measurement indicating that the general poverty level among Latinos is high. The U.S. Census data also shows that the level of poverty is most severe among children, adolescents and single female heads-of-household. This concentration of poverty among Latino children, adolescents and single female heads-of-household is troublesome given the youthful nature of the U.S. Latino population as a whole, and the increasing number of Latino families headed by single females. According to the 1996 U.S. Census, 41% of Latinos were under the age of 21 compared to 27.8% of white non-Latino persons (U.S. Department of Commerce, Bureau of the Census, 1997d).

WHAT ARE THE CAUSES OF POVERTY AMONG LATINOS?

During the past decade, social scientists have blamed the high rate of poverty among Latinos on one or all of the following factors: (1) the breakdown of the extended Latino family system (see: Garcia-Coll & Vasquez Garcia, 1995); (2) Latino cultural values such as their fatalistic view of their destinies (see Delgado, 1977, Harwood, 1977); (3) the establishment of a ghetto mentality among people living in the inner city which inhibits them from obtaining good-paying jobs (Wilson, 1996); (4) the unmotivated and unwilling attitudes of the poor to better their lives (see Harrington, 1984); and (5) Latino high unemployment rates, low high school and college graduation rates, and low rates of employment in highly-paid occupations (Perez & De la Rosa, 1993; Aponte, 1993).

The limited research available on Latino poverty indicates that the breakdown of the Latino extended family system, the fatalistic view that some Latinos have toward life and their poor motivation for bettering their lives are primarily by-products of the conditions of poverty Latinos experience and not the causes of their poverty (Suro, 1998). Instead, a small but growing body of research suggests that Latino poverty conditions are primarily the outcome of a lack of systematic access to economic and educational opportunities rather than a consequence of individual character, family conditions or cultural values (Aponte, 1993; Perez & De la Rosa, 1993). The findings from this research suggest that Latinos' high unemployment rates, low high school and college graduation rates, low income-earning levels, and low rates of employment in highly-paid occupations seem to be the primary causes of poverty among Latinos (Perez & De la Rosa, 1993; Aponte, 1993; Darby, 1996). Furthermore, the results from this research also indicate that underlying the primary causes of poverty among Latinos are the following factors: (1) the youthfulness of the Latino population; (2) the illegal immigration status of many Latinos; (3) the low educational attainment level of foreign-born Latinos before they immigrate to the U.S.; (4) the lack of English proficiency of many Latinos; and (5) the discrimination Latinos experienced because of their skin color or national origin (Suro, 1998).

The findings from this research are not surprising and, in fact, are in line with most economic historical research regarding the underlying factors responsible for poverty conditions in this country and other parts of the world. Landes' (1998) economic historical treatise on the wealth and poverty of nations documents that the primary causes of poverty in poor nations and poverty in rich nations are the inability of poor people in these nations to gain access to good education and to play a significant role in controlling the means of production and distribution of resources. Therefore, if one wants to more clearly understand why there is such a high rate of poverty among Latinos, one must first investigate in greater depth the impact of the socioeconomic factors reported by previous research.

Understanding the impact that these factors have on the poverty conditions of Latinos could result in the development of more effective social welfare programs to address the poverty conditions of this population. Exploring individual, familial and cultural explanations of poverty among Latinos, while a laudable research endeavor, in itself, should be deferred to future research inquiry as this paper's author sees it, since it seems to play a less pivotal role as a primary cause of poverty among Latinos.

This section of the paper, therefore, seeks to: (1) explore the impact of occupational status and educational attainment on Latino poverty conditions; (2) discuss the role of Latino youthfulness, immigration status, lack of English skills, and the educational attainment levels of Latino immigrants before coming to the U.S. on Latinos' high unemployment rates, low level of participation in highly-paid occupations and low educational attainment levels; and (3) explore the effects of discrimination on Latinos' poor occupational status, high unemployment rates, and low educational attainment levels.

Occupational Status and Earnings

Unemployment. Data from the U.S. Department of Labor, Bureau of Labor Statistics (1998) reveals that as of March 1998, seasonally-adjusted civilian population unemployment rates were higher among Latinos (6.9%) than white non-Latino persons (4.1%), and lower than blacks (9.2%) (Department of Labor, Bureau of Labor Statistics, 1998). It should be noted that the unemployment rates among Latinos are at a historic low level. Generally, in the past, the unemployment rates among Latinos have been higher than 8%. For example, in July of 1997, the unemployment rate for Latinos stood at 8.2% (U.S. Department of Labor, Bureau of Labor Statistics, 1998). Furthermore, data from the Bureau of Labor Statistics (1998) indicates that, despite their higher unemployment rates, Latinos had a higher rate of participation in the civilian employment population than white non-Latinos and blacks (68.6%, 67.4%, 65.8% respectively). These data suggest that, in spite of all the barriers that Latinos and blacks face, they are willing and motivated to work (Suro, 1998)

Needless to say, the high rate of unemployment among Latinos has had a deleterious impact on their poverty conditions. Data from the

1996 U.S. Census indicates that 41.1% of Latinos who did not work during 1996 lived in poverty, compared to 28.3% who worked full-time but not year-round, and 8.5% who worked year-round full-time (U.S. Department of Commerce, Bureau of the Census, 1997e). For white non-Latinos, the poverty rate was 22.7% for those who did not work during 1996, 14% for those who worked full-time but not year-round, and 2.5% for those who worked year-round full-time. Why white non-Latino unemployed persons had lower rates of poverty than Latinos is not known. However, there are several possible explanations for these results. One explanation is that the illegal immigration status that many Latinos find themselves in does not allow them to qualify for unemployment benefits and other governmental assistance which often serves as a safety net for unemployed workers while they are not working. This lack of government assistance can push more Latinos than non-Latino unemployed persons into poverty. A second possible explanation is that unemployed white non-Latino persons may have a more extensive informal support network to turn to for financial help during times of need than foreign-born Latinos. One thing is sure, more research is needed to clarify the underlying factors responsible for a higher rate of poverty among Latinos than white non-Latino persons.

Low Income and Employment in Highly-Paid Positions. Just as important as the impact that unemployment has on the poverty conditions among Latinos is the impact of Latinos' low income on these conditions (U.S. Department of Commerce, Bureau of the Census, 1997f). According to the 1996 U.S. Census, as shown in Table 3, Latino males and females had lower incomes than white non-Latino persons. More than 25% of Latino males had incomes below $10,000 and 41.2% of Latino females had incomes below $10,000. For white non-Latinos, 18.1% of males had incomes below $10,000, and 32.6% of females had incomes below $10,000 (see Table 3).

Directly associated with Latinos' low income is the employment of Latinos in highly-paid skilled and professional occupations. According to the 1996 U.S. Census (see Table 4), Latino workers were more highly concentrated than white non-Latino workers in machine operator, fabricator, labor and farming jobs (U.S. Department of Commerce, Bureau of the Census, 1997g). These jobs usually paid lower wages than managerial, professional or technical jobs where white non-Lati-

TABLE 3. Earnings of Persons by Race, Ethnicity, and Gender in 1996 (Median Earnings by Percentage)

	Latino	White
Income Level	**Male**	**Male**
Less than $10,000	25.9	18.1
$10,000 to 24,999	44.7	25.2
$25,000 to 49,999	23.0	35.0
$50,000 or more	6.4	21.7
Income Level	**Female**	**Female**
Less than $10,000	41.2	32.6
$10,000 to 24,999	41.1	35.8
$25,000 to 49,999	15.0	25.2
$50,000 or more	2.7	6.3

Source: Department of Commerce, Bureau of the Census, 1997f.

TABLE 4. Occupational Distributions by Race/Ethnicity, Employed Persons Age 16 and Over, Both Sexes (Percentages)

	All Persons	Latino	White	Black
Total	100.0	100.0	100.0	100.0
Occupation:				
Managerial and Professional	28.8	13.8	31.7	19.2
Technical, Sales and Admin. Support	30.3	24.9	31.0	29.1
Service	13.6	21.1	18.5	22.4
Precision Production, Craft and Repair	10.4	12.1	9.3	7.6
Operators, Fabricators, and Laborers	14.3	22.7	12.5	20.7
Farming, Forestry, and Fishing	2.6	5.3	2.6	0.9

Source: U.S. Department of Commerce, Bureau of the Census, 1997g.

no workers were found to be more highly concentrated than Latinos (see Table 4).

Why are Latinos more concentrated in lower-paid occupations than white non-Latino workers? Several factors may account for these occupational participation differences. First, Latinos are a youthful population. They may, therefore, not have the skills or education necessary to compete for more highly-paid jobs or to be in the labor force at all (Suro, 1998). Second, many Latinos, mostly of Mexican-American and South and Central American ancestry, are recent immigrants or are illegal immigrants (Porters & Rumbaut, 1996). Their immigration status coupled with their lack of English language proficiency may make it more difficult for them to compete in the U.S. labor market (Porters & Rumbaut, 1996). Third, discrimination barriers faced by Latinos because of their color of skin or national origin may also place them at a disadvantage in the labor force.

The explanations just given of why Latinos are more concentrated in lower-paid occupations seem to be supported by several studies of Latino immigrants. One study found that stereotypes of Mexican-American immigrants by employers as being only suitable for menial labor jobs affected both their earnings and participation in more highly-paid jobs (Lieberson & Waters, 1987). A second study of Latino immigrants found that with more Latinos arriving from countries such as the Dominican Republic who have darker skin color, racial discrimination at work against this new group of Latino immigrants has increased (Suro, 1998). More importantly, research on the poverty conditions of Latinos has shown that the educational attainment of Latinos may be the biggest underlying factor responsible for the disparity in occupational status and income-earnings between Latinos and white non-Latinos. The impact of Latino educational attainment levels on their occupational status and income-earning levels is discussed in detail below.

Educational Attainment

No one factor has had a stronger impact on Latino poverty condition than their educational attainment levels. In fact, one could argue that the low educational attainment of Latinos is largely responsible for Latinos' low income-earnings, high unemployment levels and low participation in highly-paid skill or professional occupations. Data from the 1996 U.S. Census shows that poverty and educational attainment are inextricably linked (U.S. Department of Commerce, Bureau of the Census, 1997h). These data support the findings from previous research which documents the fact that persistent and severe poverty leads to lower levels of educational attainment among Latinos and non-Latino adolescents (Duncan & Brooks-Gunn, 1997). The U.S. Census data also supports the findings from research which has concluded that low educational attainment leads to higher poverty rates among adults (Kelso, 1994). The U.S. Census data presented in this section of the paper will primarily focus on documenting the impact of low educational attainment on the impoverished conditions of Latino adults. The U.S. Census data documenting the impact of poverty on adolescent Latinos' educational attainment will be presented in the "Consequences" section of this paper.

Educational Attainment Among Latinos 25 Years Old and Older. The 1996 U.S. Census indicates that 54.7% of Latinos 25 years old and older have graduated from high school, compared to 86.3% of white non-Latino persons, and 75.3% of black persons (U.S. Department of Commerce, Bureau of the Census, 1997i). The 1996 U.S. Census data on educational attainment among Latino subgroups further indicates that Mexican-Americans 25 years and older had much lower high school graduation completion rates (48.6%) than Cubans (65.2%), Puerto Ricans (61.1%), and South and Central Americans (63.2%). Finally, trend data from the U.S. Census is also in agreement that similar or slightly lower high school graduation completion rates among Latinos prevailed during the 1980s and early 1990s.

Why are there significant differences in the high school graduation completion rates between Mexican-Americans and the other Latino subgroups? Although the answer to this question is not known, Portes and Rumbaut (1996), two well-known researchers on Latino immigration, have hypothesized that there may be several factors which account for these differences. First, a higher percentage of Cubans and South and Central American adults, with the exception of Salvadorans, who immigrated to the United States in the past two decades, were better-educated than Mexican-American immigrants before coming to the United States. Second, unlike Mexican-American immigrants, Cubans and the majority of South and Central Americans who immigrate to the United States come to this country legally or as political refugees with legal immigration status. The legal immigration status of adult Cuban and South and Central American immigrants allows them better access than Mexican-Americans to educational opportunities in the United States (e.g., completing high school education, qualifying for postsecondary financial aid, job training programs, etc.).

Regarding the higher graduation rates of Puerto Ricans than Mexican-Americans, Fitzpatrick (1987), a well-known researcher of Puerto Rican migration, argues that the primary reason why a higher percentage of Puerto Ricans graduate from high school than Mexican-Americans is because attending high school is compulsory in Puerto Rico and not in Mexico. As the result of the Puerto Ricans' government educational policy toward compulsory education, many more Puerto Rican persons who were born in Puerto Rico and moved to the mainland United States have completed their high school education than Mexican-Americans who immigrated to the United States (Fitzpatrick, 1987). Puerto Rico as a territory of the United States adheres to this country's laws and regulations regarding compulsory school attendance.

Educational Attainment and Poverty Among Latinos 25 Years Old or Older. Overall, data from the 1996 U.S. Census, as shown in Table 5, indicates that Latinos 25 years old or older who did not have a high school diploma were more than six times as likely to live in poverty

TABLE 5. Poverty Status in 1996 of Persons 25 Years and Older by Race/Ethnicity and Years of School Completed (Percentages)

	Latino	White	Black
Educational Level			
No High School Diploma	33.9	21.8	39.5
High School Diploma- No College	15.6	8.3	21.2
Some College- No BA or Higher Degree	11.6	5.9	12.6
Completed BA or Higher Degree	5.7	3.6	3.7

Source: U.S. Department of Commerce, Bureau of the Census, 1997i.

than Latinos who completed a Bachelor of Arts or higher educational degree (U.S. Department of Commerce, Bureau of the Census, 1997i). In addition, as shown in Table 5, Latinos 25 years or older, regardless of educational attainment levels, had higher poverty rates than white non-Latino persons. Blacks, however, who did not have high school diplomas, had higher poverty rates than either Latino or white non-Latino persons.

As readers will notice, the 1996 Census data provides evidence of a strong relationship between Latinos' educational attainment levels and their high poverty rates. These data also raise several questions in need of additional research: Why is it that white non-Latino persons who have not obtained a high school diploma, are high school graduates, or have some college education, have lower poverty rates than their Latino counterparts? Are these poverty rate differences due to racial discrimination experienced by Latinos when obtaining employment? Or to the illegal immigration status of many Latinos which does not allow them the opportunity to obtain employment even though they may be more highly educated than white non-Latino persons? Or to their lack of English proficiency? While little empirical evidence exists to answer these questions, anecdotal information from several studies suggests that the higher poverty rates among Latinos than white non-Latino persons without a high school diploma may be due to forces in the labor market that further marginalize the most marginal of Latinos (Suro, 1998).

These studies suggest that Mexican-American illegal immigrants who speak little or no English and have no high school education are funneled to work in menial jobs that pay below the minimum wage with no possibility of upward economic mobility. In contrast, although white non-Latino persons without high school diplomas also experience serious difficulties in obtaining employment, they seem to have fewer difficulties than Latinos or blacks in securing stable employment in menial jobs that pay at least the minimum wage by the time they are in their mid-twenties (Wilson, 1996).

The data from the 1996 U.S. Census also raises an additional question. Why is it that Puerto Ricans' poverty rates are higher than Mexican-American rates even though the high school graduation completion rates among Puerto Ricans age 25 and older are higher than those of Mexican-Americans? Are these poverty rates due to a higher percentage of single female heads-of-household among Puerto Ricans than Mexican-Americans? Or due to the greater availability of lower-paying menial jobs in rural areas where many Mexican-Americans live than in urban areas where most Puerto Ricans live?

The findings from several reports suggest that because of the responsibilities associated with solo parenting, many Puerto Rican female heads-of-household who are high school graduates are unable to hold a job, which often places them in poverty (National Council of La Raza, 1995). Often these female heads-of-household have to resort to government assistance to provide for their children. The cash assistance that they received from the federal and state government in the form of payments under such welfare programs as Temporary Assistance to Needy Families program (TANF), formerly known as Aid to Families for Dependent Children (AFDC), is often not enough to pull them above the poverty threshold (National Council of la Raza, 1997).

Similarly, several studies suggest that the availability of more low-paying menial jobs in rural areas in the Southwest where many Mexican-Americans live than in urban areas in the Northeast where the majority of Puerto Ricans live may account for the lower poverty rates among Mexican-Americans than Puerto Ricans (Suro, 1998). Most of the menial jobs available to Mexican-Americans are farming or laborer jobs which require no high school education or English-speaking ability. On the other hand, many of the menial jobs available to Puerto Ricans require some level of English fluency and in many instances a high school diploma (Suro, 1998). Whether the above-mentioned factors are responsible for the higher poverty rates among Puerto Ricans than Mexican Americans despite Puerto Ricans higher high school graduation completion rates remains to be further explored.

THE CONSEQUENCES OF POVERTY: WHAT ARE THE EFFECTS ON THE WELL-BEING OF LATINOS?

Data from national surveys and research studies are now providing information on the effects of poverty on the well-being of Latinos (see for example: De la Rosa, 1989; Report of the Secretary's Department of Health and Human Service Task Force on Black and Minority Health, 1985; U.S. Department of Commerce, Bureau of the Census, 1997b). The findings from this research provide evidence that there is a relationship between poverty and the low educational attainment of

Latino children and youth (Duncan & Brooks-Gunn, 1997). Other research has also documented the effects of poverty on the health status of Latinos (JAMA, 1991). This next section of the paper will address the impact that poverty has on the educational attainment of Latino children and adolescents and the health status of all Latinos.

Poverty and Educational Attainment: Tomorrow's Poor

Effects of Poverty on Latino Children's Educational Achievement. During the past decade, research has documented the impact of poverty on children's and adolescents' educational attainment (see for example: Huston, 1991; Chase-Lansdale & Brooks-Gunn, 1995; Fitzgerald, Lester, & Zuckerman, 1995; Conger, Jewsbury-Conger, & Elder, 1997, Duncan & Brooks-Gunn, 1997). This research found that black and white non-Latino children who live in persistent and severe poverty were less likely to perform well in school as measured by reading and math test scores for children (Smith, Brooks-Gunn, & Klebanov, 1997). Unfortunately, comparable data for Latino children does not exist. Researchers who have analyzed data from studies such as the National Longitudinal Survey of Youth (NLSY) and the Infant Health and Development Project (IHDP) have excluded Latino children from their analysis because many of the academic achievement measurements were not administered in Spanish (Smith, Brooks-Gunn, & Klebanov, 1997). This problem in measurement has resulted in missing data in some cases and English assessment for bilingual but primarily Spanish-speaking children in other cases. Nevertheless, anecdotal information from studies on poor Latino children suggests that poverty conditions affect their ability to learn (Garcia-Coll & Vasquez-Garcia, 1995). Poor Latino children are less likely to do well in school than Latino children who don't face poverty.

Effects of Poverty on Latino Adolescents' Educational Achievement. On the other hand, there is more data available detailing the effects of poverty on the educational attainment of Latino adolescents and young adults. Data from the 1996 U.S. Census, as shown in Table 6, indicates that 29.4% of Latinos ages 16-24 drop out[1] of school compared to 13% of blacks, and 7.3% of white non-Latino persons ages 16-24 (U.S. Department of Commerce, Bureau of the Census, 1997j). Further, the 1996 U.S. census data, as shown in Table 6, make the case that Latinos, ages 16-24, whose families had low income-earning levels, had dropout rates almost four times as high as Latinos

TABLE 6. Status Dropout Rate, Ages 16-24, by Income and Race/Ethnicity: October 1996 (Percentages)

		Race/Ethnicity[1]		
	All Persons	**White Non-Latino**	**Black Non-Latino**	**Latino**
Family Income[2]				
	11.1	7.3	13.0	29.4
Low income level	22.1	13.9	21.9	42.4
Middle income level	10.8	8.3	9.0	24.9
High income level	2.6	2.0	2.5	11.0

[1]Due to relatively small sample sizes, American Indian/Alaskan Natives and Asian/Pacific Islanders are included in the total but are not shown separately.

[2]Low income is defined as the bottom 20 percent of all family incomes for 1996; middle income is between 20 and 80 percent of all family incomes; and high income is the top 20 percent of all families.

Source: U.S. Department of Commerce, Bureau of the Census, Current Population Survey, 1997j.

whose families had high income-earning levels. Also white and black non-Latinos ages 16-24 whose families had low income-earning levels had much higher dropout rates than black and white non-Latino persons whose families had high income-earning levels (see Table 6).

While the high school dropout rates among Latinos may not be due to their poverty conditions alone, it is apparent that poverty does have a significant impact on the dropout rates of Latino adolescents and young adults. Other factors which may have an impact on Latino adolescents and young adults high school dropout rates are their nativity status (i.e., foreign or U.S. born) and ability to speak English (see for example: Bennici & Strang, 1995; Strang, Winglee, & Stunkard, 1993). The 1995 Census data shows that over half of the foreign-born Latinos who were counted as dropouts never enrolled in school, and 80% of these young adults reported as speaking English either "not well" or "not at all" (Mcmillen, Kaufman, & Klein, 1997). Not surprisingly, these high school dropout rates leave a significant number of Latino youth ill-prepared to compete for highly-paid skilled or technical jobs in today's economy. As a result, many of these dropouts eventually join the ranks of the poor, becoming trapped in a cycle of poverty with little opportunity for upward economic mobility. Ten years from now, the cycle will be repeated again as the children of today's dropouts become tomorrow's dropouts and tomorrow's poor.

Health Status

Since the U.S. Secretary of Health and Human Services released the Task Force Report on Black and Minority Health in 1985, there has been some epidemiologic research conducted on the health status of Latinos (U.S. Department of Health and Human Services, 1985; De La Rosa, 1989; JAMA, 1991). The data from this research as detailed in an executive summary of the editorial board of JAMA (1991) suggests that the health status of Latinos is below that of white non-Latinos. Yet, despite a growing body of research documenting Latinos poor health status, the editorial board of JAMA also concluded that few studies exist that document the association between Latinos' poor economic status and their health status (JAMA, 1991). Included below is a broad overview of the findings from some the few studies which have documented the relationship between the poverty conditions of Latinos and their health status.

Low Birth Weight. Research on the effects of poverty on the low birth weight of Latino women has not been able to fully assess the impact that poverty conditions have on the low birth weights of Latino infants. While researchers know that Latino women who live in poverty, who are younger, and unmarried are at higher risk of giving birth to infants with low birth weights, they have not yet be able to determine how significant a role poverty plays in the low birth weights. The few studies which have been conducted on this subject offer contradictory findings (Roberts, 1997; Shiono et al., 1997). Roberts (1997) found that the poverty conditions of Latino and black women had a greater effect on their risk of having children with low birth weight than their age and marital status. On the other hand, Shiono et al. (1997) found marital status and maternal age to be more strongly associated with the low birth weight of Latino, black, white non-Latino and Chinese infants than their poverty conditions. What seems to be clear is that Latino women who utilize prenatal care more often are less likely to have infants with low birth weight. The higher utilization of prenatal care by some Latino women has been attributed by researchers to their better socioeconomic status, higher level of education and higher health insurance coverage (Ginzberg, 1991).

Substance Abuse. The effects of poverty on Latino substance abuse also remain not fully understood in spite of the fact that data from several national surveys indicate that substance abuse is a serious problem for Latino adults and adolescents (De La Rosa, 1998). In fact, evidence from the 1995 National Household Survey on Drug Abuse (NHSDA) and the 1996-97 Monitoring the Future Study (MTF) leads to the conclusion that adolescent Latinos had higher drug use rates than their black and white non-Latino counterparts for a number of the most dangerous drugs: cocaine, crack cocaine and powder cocaine, and heroin (Substance Abuse and Mental Health Administration, 1997; Johnston et al., in press).

The few studies which exist are now providing evidence regarding the connection between poverty and Latinos' substance abuse behavior. One study by Vega, Gil and Wagner (1998) found that Latino adolescents who were the most marginalized from American society had the highest rate of drug use initiation and continued experimentation among Latino adolescents. On the other hand, Latino adolescents who were culturally well integrated into American society had the lowest rate of drug use. A second study by Bourgois (1995) found that Latino drug use and dealing was inextricably linked to their economic conditions in the *barrio.*

HIV/AIDS. Remaining to be explored is the impact that living in poverty has on becoming infected with HIV/AIDS among Latinos. This dearth of research persists despite the fact that the problem of HIV/AIDS is a serious problem among Latinos. According to the Center for Disease Control (CDC), in 1994, nearly 21% of all AIDS cases reported in 1994 among females were Latinas. Among males, 14% of all reported AIDS case in 1994 were Latinos (Center for Disease Control, 1994). These rates of AIDS cases among Latinos are disproportionate to the percentage of Latinos living in the mainland United States.

As with substance abuse, the few studies which have examined the effects of poverty on the HIV/AIDS rates of Latinos indicate that a strong relationship exists between poverty conditions and the risk of exposure to HIV/AIDS among Latinos. An ethnographic study by Singer (1994) found that the majority of Latino injecting drug users with AIDS lived in poverty conditions before their illness was diagnosed. While other factors such as family drug use and peer drug use influenced the drug habits of Latino injecting drug users, the lack of economic opportunity played an equally important role in their adoption of drug-using lifestyles. Once involved in this lifestyle, many injecting drug users find it hard to leave their habit. Even those who want to reduce or stop their drug use are prevented from doing so by their lack of health insurance coverage or access to appropriate drug treatment programs (Singer, 1994).

Diabetes. Similarly, there is a paucity of data regarding the effects of poverty on one of the leading causes of death among Latinos: diabetes (JAMA, 1991). How poverty conditions are related to the high rate of diabetes among Latinos remains to be more fully examined. What seems to be clear from the information currently available is that poorer Latinos seem to have higher rates of diabetes than the rest of the Latino population. One study documenting the diabetes rates of poor Latinas found the prevalence of diabetes to be four times higher than that of the total Latino population (Stern, 1984). The study's author as well as other researchers attribute the high rate of diabetes among Latinos, particularly the poor, directly to the high prevalence of obesity found among Latinos (JAMA, 1991).

Cancer. On the other hand, more data does exist regarding the relationship between poverty and cancer than on AIDS, substance abuse, or diabetes among Latinos. Data from the National Cancer Database provides the information that Latinos with income levels below $13,500 were more than three times as likely as Latinos with incomes above $22,000 to report having being diagnosed with cancer (Villar & Menck, 1994). In another study, Elder et al. (1991) found that less acculturated Latinos, many of whom were presumed to have lower incomes, were at higher risk of being diagnosed with cancer than more acculturated Latinos, many of whom were presumed to have higher incomes. Why Latinos who are poorer are more likely to have higher risk of being diagnosed with cancer may be associated with one or more of the following possibilities: (1) lack of insurance to screen for cancer; (2) inferior diet; (3) living in neighborhoods with hazardous environmental conditions; (4) lack of education or fluency in English, thus preventing the Latino citizen from obtaining needed information on cancer-prevention activities; and (5) fear of going to physicians for screening because of illegal immigration status.

Heart Disease. There is also a dearth of research linking the poverty status of Latinos with their risk of heart disease. However, several studies conducted in the 1980s conclude that poor Latinos exhibit higher risk for unrecognized and untreated hypertension (Munoz, Lecca, & Goldstein, 1988; Kumanyika, Savage, & Ramirez, 1989). Overall, hypertension is more prevalent among Latinos than white non-Latinos (JAMA, 1991). Why poorer Latinos have higher risk of hypertension may be related to their lack of insurance, poorer diet, living in neighborhoods where levels of stress may be high because of the high level of violence or drug dealing, or other unknown environmental or genetic factors.

REDUCING POVERTY AMONG LATINOS: A PLAN OF ACTION

While there continues to be a dearth of research on the effects of poverty on the well-being of Latinos, the information available provides a grim picture of poverty's devastating impact. This information suggests that there is a growing Latino underclass in this country. With the presence of Latinos growing in the U.S., the negative impact of a large Latino underclass is sure to be felt in the future beyond the Latino neighborhoods. As people from the baby boom generation begin to retire in the next decade, the U.S. economy will rely more on the younger Latino population to replace them.

Importance of a Plan of Action to Reduce Latino Poverty

Unfortunately, if the present conditions of Latino impoverishment persist, the younger Latinos will not be able to replace retiring baby boomers: they will not have the technical skills or educational background required by the highly skilled technical or professional positions left behind by the retiring baby boomers. This inability of Latinos to replace baby boomers in the labor force could have negative implications for the private and public sector of the U.S. economy. In the public sector, first of all, the U.S. government may not be able to collect enough revenue in the form of taxes to maintain the current social infrastructure including paying Social Security benefits to retired baby boomers. At the same time, policy makers at the state and federal level will be faced with increasing spending to deal with the growing problem of poverty among Latinos. In the private sector, large and small companies may be saddled with high expenses associated with their efforts to recruit highly educated and skilled foreigners or to train an unskilled Latino labor force.

Rationale for the Proposed Plan of Action

For policy makers to avoid such a scenario from occurring, they need to develop a plan of action that will educate Latinos, provide economic development in Latino communities, and assist those Latinos with the greatest economic need. This plan of action should be based on the premise that poverty is not due to some individual flaw or cultural tradition but to inequalities in our social and economic system. Many of the ideas proposed under this plan are not new. In fact, they are based upon past programs and ideas that have proven to be effective when appropriately implemented and funded. While this country's current political and economic climate may lead one to believe that it will be unlikely that some of the recommendations listed in this paper will ever become a reality, some recent changes in the political and economic landscape make the implementation of the recommendations which have been listed in this paper more realistic.

On the political front, Latinos and other minority groups such as blacks are beginning to have a greater impact in this country's electoral process. For example, during the 1998 congressional and statewide elections more Latinos and blacks were elected to political office than ever before (Purdum, 1998; Sack, 1998). In fact, many Republican and Democratic political experts attributed the Democratic Party's strong showing in the 1998 elections to the high voter turnout of Latinos and blacks (Purdum, 1998; Sack, 1998). Many Latinos and blacks, spurred by the racist and divisive policies of the Republican Party toward minority groups, have begun to organize more effectively in an effort to overturn some of the recent defeats in affirmative action programs with the passage of such state ballots' initiatives as proposition 187 in California. It is this author's belief that the increasing political power of minority populations will have a spill-over effect in the years to come regarding the development and implementation of social welfare and educational programs which will address the poverty conditions faced by Latinos and blacks.

On the economic front, the big federal government budget surpluses expected to be generated by this country in the next fifteen years could provide the resources necessary for the development and implementation of some of the welfare, employment and educational programs listed in this paper's recommendations. According to some estimates, in the next fifteen years the federal government is expected to generate budget surpluses exceeding four trillion dollars (*New York Times*, 1999). While it is expected that some of the money from the budget surpluses will go to shore up the Social Security program or be used for tax cuts, it is also conceivable that given the rising political power of minority populations, some of the budget surpluses might be used to fund programs that would reduce poverty among Latinos and blacks.

This idea to use money from future budget surpluses to fund poverty programs is not without controversy and in fact is in direct contradiction to the Clinton administration's current welfare policy objective which is to reduce the federal government involvement in social welfare programs for the poor. In addition, this idea of more federal government involvement in social welfare programs for the poor runs counter to the current public sentiment that the plight of the poor is not the federal government's responsibility. In fact, the current American public sentiment toward the poor is that the poor should take care of themselves and not rely on any government handouts.

However, it is this author's contention that this conservative approach toward dealing with the plight of the poor in America will probably begin to shift to a more liberal approach within the next ten years. The increase in Latino and black political power, the ever-growing political and economic power of white non-Latino women who tend to favor the funding of domestic programs over defense spending, and the availability of resources to fund programs for the poor will spark a new era of more direct federal government intervention in addressing poverty conditions among poor people. This new era is not hard to envision if one follows recent political forecasts that are based upon demographic changes in the U.S. populations which suggest that blacks, Latinos and white non-Latino women are expected to comprise about 70% of the electorate by the year 2010 (Purdum, 1998). This large shift in the make-up of the U.S. electorate will have major political ramifications which could lead to radical changes in the federal government's social welfare programs toward the poor in the next fifty years.

This potential swing of the pendulum from a conservative to a liberal ideology regarding this country's social welfare polices toward the poor is not without historical precedent. During the 20th century, the U.S. government's social welfare policies toward the poor have swung from a conservative to a liberal ideology about every thirty-five to forty years (Danziger, 1989). Witness the federal government swings in ideology in social welfare policies toward the poor during the periods of 1900-1935, 1935-75, and 1975 to the present (Ginsberg, 1996; Danziger, 1989). Each of these periods has been preceded by a change in the political order as it was during the 1930s with the rise of the Democratic Party to political power, and in the late 1970s with the rise of the Republican party to political power (Ginsberg, 1996).

During the period between 1900 and 1935, the federal government approach toward the poor was one of non-involvement. The federal government felt that the poor had to be responsible for themselves and social policy and programs for the poor were the province of state and local government and charities. Beginning in 1935 and ending about 1975, there was a major shift in the federal government's social welfare policy for the poor. The federal government through the New Deal and Great Society federal legislative initiatives became more actively involved in eradicating poverty (Ginsberg, 1996). In fact, there was a general belief by the federal government that the problem of poverty and hunger in American society could be solved. This period of active federal government involvement ended around the late 1970s with the rise in American society of public sentiment in favor of the federal government's limiting its direct involvement in the amelioration of poverty (Ginsberg, 1996).

The election of Reagan and his administration's New Federalism legislative agenda which drastically reduced the federal government's involvement in social welfare programs for the poor solidified the swing toward a more conservative ideology toward the poor. The conservative stance was further solidified in the early 1990s with the Republican party wins in the 1994 U.S. Congressional election and its Contract with America legislative agenda which was codified into law with the passage of 1996 Personal Responsibility and Work Opportunity Act legislation (Ginsberg, 1996). While no changes are expected in the next five years in the federal government current policy toward the poor, it is this author's contention that we are at the end of another conservative era in this country's social welfare policies toward the poor and at the doorstep of a new more liberal era in this country's approach regarding their plight. This liberal era will make it more likely that the recommendations which are made in this paper for reducing poverty among Latinos will become reality.

The Proposed Plan of Action

Included below are several recommendations which this author believes should be included in any serious plan of action by the federal government to reduce poverty among Latinos. However, before proceeding with the text of the recommendations, a comment needs to be made about the recommendations. These recommendations have been limited to Latinos because the focus of the paper is on Latino poverty. Obviously these recommendations can also be used to develop a plan of action to address the poverty conditions of all poor people in America. In fact, an argument could be made that a plan of action that includes this paper's recommendations in its search to address the problem of poverty among all poor people rather than just the Latino poor will be more effective in achieving its goals.

Educational Assistance and Development. The federal government must take a more active role in providing the resources necessary to build schools and educational programs in Latino communities that can stem the high school dropout rates among Latinos. The federal government can do this by providing more funding to the Head Start program. This funding can be used to increase the number of Latino children receiving assistance through Head Start at the elementary and junior high school levels. Additional educational programs should be developed to identify and help academically at-risk children from falling further behind in their reading, math and science skills. These programs should seek to involve the parents or significant others of the children and adolescents.

At the high school level, educational programs geared toward helping Latino youth at risk of dropping out should be developed. These programs should provide both financial and academic assistance to youth at risk of dropping out. Efforts should be undertaken to once again expand the Upward Bound Program to help struggling Latino youth obtain admission to colleges and universities, and to help them complete their college degrees. For those Latino youth who drop out from school, alternative learning centers located in Latino communities should be developed and staffed with quality teachers. The mission of these alternative learning centers will be to help the school dropouts obtain their high school equivalency diplomas (GEDs) or to help them return to school to obtain their high school diploma.

These school dropout programs should offer stipends to help lure school dropouts into the classroom. Many Latino youth drop out of school in order to hold menial jobs or to be employed in the illegal economy. They do it, in part, to help their families. Many may not return to school unless they see an immediate financial incentive to return. Extensive child care should also be provided to allow single mothers who are school dropouts to return to school. Many of these single mothers may not return to school unless they know they have appropriate child care.

In addition, the federal government with the help of state governments should seek to develop educational programs for adult Latinos. These programs should focus on helping adult Latinos gain English proficiency and obtain their GED. A secondary aim of these programs will be to teach adult Latinos the vocational skills needed to obtain well-paying jobs. At the post-graduate college level, the federal government should establish a well-endowed fellowship program modeled after the Hispanic Scholarship Fund in order to help Latino college graduates continue their education. Many studies have shown that Latino college graduates do not continue their postgraduate education because of a lack of resources. Finally, at the postdoctoral level, federal agencies such as the National Institutes of Health (NIH) and the National Science Foundation (NSF) should increase the funding levels for minority postdoctoral fellowship and training programs. To date, only a small percentage of the NIH and NSF annual budget is set aside to fund minority fellowships and training programs.

Economic Development. The federal government in partnership with the private sector should become actively involved in expanding the economic infrastructure of poor Latino communities. The federal government, first of all, needs to expand its Small Business Administration (SBA) programs in order to become aggressively involved in reaching out to minority owned businesses in poor Latino communities. The SBA should make more loans available to Latino businesses located in poor Latino communities with financial conditions which will allow the small businesses in these communities to apply and pay for these loans. Second, the federal government should establish a grant-in-aid program that will encourage Latinos to develop new businesses that expand on existing community activities such as community gardens. These new businesses could employ community people already involved in such activities.

Third, the federal government should implement the 1992 Enterprise Zone Act in all Latino communities where the poverty rate is above 20%. The purpose of the 1992 Enterprise Zone Act was to promote business development in poor communities with a poverty rate of at least 45%. As enacted into law, the primary incentive of the Enterprise Zone Act was to provide tax breaks for businesses located outside the communities that wanted to invest in new or existing business within the designated poor communities. Under this act, for a business to be designated an "enterprise zone" business, it had to be located in the zone and conduct much of its activity within the zone. In addition, the act stipulated that one third of its employees would have to be residents of the zone. If fully implemented in Latino communities with poverty rates above 20%, the Enterprise Zone Act could lead to economic growth in minority communities, which in turn could pull many Latinos living in these communities out of poverty.

Fourth, the federal government should provide grants to Latino persons living below the U.S. poverty threshold to purchase their own homes. This program could help to: (1) spur the construction industry to create new jobs in the community; (2) establish a resident population which has a stake in the community's social and economic well-being; and (3) help to solve the serious housing problem faced by poor Latinos as well as the problem of homelessness.

Cash Transfer Payment Programs. While politically controversial, the federal government should institute a cash transfer payment program that will provide monthly cash assistance to all Latino persons and families living below the poverty threshold. This program will ensure that all working poor persons and non-working poor persons receive cash assistance equal to 150% of the poverty threshold established by the U.S. government every year. For example, the 1998 poverty threshold established by the U.S. government for a family of four was $16,450 (Federal Register, 1998).

Therefore, if this program were to be in existence in 1998, a family of four persons with no income would receive a yearly cash assistance in the amount of $24,675. For a family of four persons with income above the poverty threshold, the yearly cash assistance will depend on the income of the family. For example, if the head of the household makes $11,000 per year, this family will receive cash assistance in the amount of $13,675. In addition to the cash assistance, working single parents or couples with children at home would receive an additional stipend equal to 30% of the poverty threshold to cover child care and other work-related expenses such as transportation. In the case of a working single parent or couples, this stipend would amount to $7,402 per year.

It should be noted that, under this program, working single parents or couples who exceeded the poverty threshold income would still be eligible for cash assistance for child care and other work-related expenses. The amount would depend on their income level. Any working single parent or couple making more than $32,077 would not be eligible for child care or work-related cash assistance.

Single non-disabled unemployed males under the age of 62 would also be eligible to receive cash assistance under this program. These males would be eligible to receive cash assistance payment for a continuous period of up to three years. However, to remain eligible to receive benefits beyond these three years, these candidates for assistance would have to show initiative in seeking employment or in obtaining the skills necessary to become gainfully employed. Case workers would evaluate the eligibility of the men for this program on an individual basis. A supplementary point: the yearly cash assistance ceiling would be raised in cities or areas of the country where the cost of living is particularly high. The yearly cash assistance ceiling for these cities and areas will be set every year by the U.S. Department of Commerce in consultation with organizations and groups representing the rights of the poor.

Health Insurance Coverage. The lack of health insurance coverage among Latinos is one of the biggest factors affecting the health status of poor Latinos. Efforts need to be undertaken by the federal government to provide health insurance coverage to Latinos currently uninsured. The Medicaid program should be expanded to provide insurance to working poor Latinos who have incomes which are 150% above the current poverty threshold. In addition, the federal government should provide health insurance to unemployed Latinos who qualify for unemployment benefits by providing state unemployment offices with financial assistance to cover such insurance coverage. Finally, efforts must be made to revive the Clinton administration's health reform proposals to provide health insurance coverage to every American who does not have such coverage.

STRATEGIES FOR IMPLEMENTING
THE RECOMMENDATIONS

None of this paper's recommendations can become a reality unless Latino leaders are able to politically mobilize and bring to the forefront of American society the plight of the Latino poor. For Latino leaders to effectively mobilize, they need to develop political strategies that access the growing political power of Latinos and those friendly to the plight of poor people in America. Included below are several strategies that Latino leaders can use to effectively force the federal government to develop and implement programs that would lead to a reduction in Latino poverty.

Development of a Political Action Committee

Latino leaders from national organizations such as the National Council of La Raza, the National Puerto Rican Forum, the National Coalition of Hispanic Health and Human Services Organizations and Providers, the Southwest Voter Registration Organization, and the Mexican American Legal Defense and Educational Fund need to come together to develop a Political Action Committee (PAC) that will have as its primary aim the problem of Latino poverty. (It should be noted that because of lack of space in this paper numerous Latino national organizations and political groups are not included in the text.)

This PAC will have a variety of functions. One will be to raise funds to support current members of the U.S. Congress who support social welfare policies that benefit the poor and to defeat opponents of such policies. Funds will also be raised to supports potential members of Congress (Latino or non-Latino) who are supportive of a federal government domestic agenda which supports the recommendations listed in this paper. A second function of the PAC will be to organize Latino leaders at the local and state level to publicize through the news media and other information channels such as the Internet the plight of poor Latinos in their respective communities, cities or states.

Coalition Building

If Latino leaders who are the organizers of a movement to reduce poverty among Latinos should form a coalition with Latino elected officials and non-Latino political groups and organizations which have as their primary missions the amelioration of poverty in the country, they will be more effective. Such a coalition should include members of the U.S. Congress Hispanic Congressional Caucus and the U.S. Congress Black Congressional Caucus, the National Association of Social Workers, the Urban League, The National Association for the Advancement of Colored People (NAACP), women's rights organizations and welfare rights groups. This coalition should demand that action be taken by the federal government to address the plight of all poor people in this country.

Once organized, this coalition of elected representatives and those organizations friendly to the cause of the poor should hold a national summit on poverty followed by regional conferences to publicize the condition of America's poor. High-ranking members of the government including the President of the United States should be invited to attend and speak at the summit and regional conferences.

In addition, one of the primary functions of the coalition and the PAC should be to lobby the political party in control of the White House to have more Latinos, blacks, women, and individuals concerned with the impoverished appointed to influential governmental policy positions. Appointment of these individuals could influence the course of policy-making regarding the development and implementation of programs designed to improve the conditions of the poor in this country.

Political Drive to Register and Educate Latinos and Non-Latinos Concerned About the Status of the Poor

At the same time that elected government officials and organizations sympathetic to the conditions of the poor are working to publicize their plight, efforts should be undertaken to develop a plan of action to register Latinos and non-Latinos supportive of this cause of the poor to vote. Following the example of the Southwest Voter Registration organization, local Latino and black grassroots organizations need to organize to register more Latinos and blacks and others supportive of this cause to vote, and to get them to the polls on election day.

Rally in Washington to Highlight the Plight of the Poor

Modeling their campaign on recent major rallies on behalf of the plight of black males and gay civil rights, Latino leaders and their friends should organize a major rally in Washington to publicize the plight of Latino poor and all other poor people in America. High-ranking members of the government including the President of the United States should be invited to attend and speak at the summit and regional conferences. This major rally should be followed by a series of regional rallies in different parts of the country.

Lobbying Individual Federal Agencies to Appoint More Latinos and Non-Latinos Sensitive to the Plight of the Poor

At the same time that Latino leaders lobby the White House to appoint more Latinos and others who are concerned with the plight of the poor in America, Latino leaders and their friends should approach individual federal government agencies to increase the number of Latino middle-level government officials. Appointing Latinos into middle-level federal government positions in the federal bureaucracy will be crucial to the successful implementation of any federal government legislation which might be passed to address the plight of the Latino poor. Often middle-level federal government officials are gatekeepers who can help or hinder the implementation of legislative initiatives by the mere fact that they control important information, and, often the resources needed to implement such policies.

Seeking Funding for Research on Latino Poverty

Latino leaders and their allies need to seek funding from the federal government to conduct additional research on the impact that poverty has on the well-being of Latinos. The findings from this research could be utilized by Latino leaders and their allies to further bolster their claims regarding the devastating impact that poverty has on the lives of poor Latinos. This information should be publicized through all the major news media channels as further evidence that programs such as those listed in this paper's recommendations should be implemented to reduce the pain and suffering of poor Latinos.

CONCLUSION

As we enter the 21st century, a significant percentage of Latinos continue to live in poverty. Even though the presence of Latinos is becoming more prominent in the social, economic, and political life of the country, the condition of impoverishment faced by a large segment of the Latino population can have a detrimental effect on the future well-being of the United States both economically and socially. Demographic projections indicate that by the year 2020 there will be 60 million Latinos living in the United States with more than 60% younger than age 25. By the year 2050, demographic projections indicate that there will be close to 120 million Latinos living in this country (U.S. Department Bureau of the Census, 1997a). This major demographic shift in the U.S. population in the next fifty years will have severe cultural, economic, political and social implications for this country. The U.S. must be prepared to respond to this major shift in the population. Central to this response is the development of policies and programs that will confront the underlying causes of poverty and related consequences for Latinos. Failure to do so could lead to major economic and social upheaval of far greater cost to this country than the resources allocated to address the economic needs of today's Latino population.

NOTE

1. In this paper, the status dropout rates measure was used rather than the event or cohort rates measure reported by the U.S. Census to measure Latino school dropout rates. The status dropout rate was selected because it provides a much broader view of the dropout school problem. According to the U.S. Census status dropout rates provide cumulative data on dropouts among adolescents and young adults within a specified age range. Event rates describe the proportion of students who leave school each year without completing a high school program and cohort rates measure what happens to a cohort of students over a period of time. Status rates are higher than events because they include all dropouts, regardless of when they last attended school. In addition, status rates also can reveal more accurately the extent of the dropout problem in a given population group.

REFERENCES

Aponte, R. (1993). Hispanic families in poverty: Diversity, context, and interpretation. *Families in Society, 74*(9), 527-537.

Bennici, F., & Strang, W. (1995). *An analysis of language minority and limited English proficient students from NELS: 88.* Washington, D.C.: U.S. Department of Education.

Bourgois, P. (1995). *In search of respect: Selling crack in el barrio.* Cambridge, MA: Cambridge University Press.

Brooks-Gunn, J., Klebanov, P., Liaw, F., & Duncan, G. (1995). Toward an understanding of the effects of poverty upon children. In H. E. Fitzgerald, B. M. Lester, & B. Zuckerman (Eds.), *Children of poverty: Research, health, and policy* (pp. 3-41). New York: Garland Publishing, Inc.

Centers for Disease Control and Prevention. (June, 1994). *HIV/AIDS surveillance report.* Volume 6, Number 1. Washington, DC: U.S. Government Printing Office.

Chase-Landsdale, P. L., & Brooks-Gunn, J. (1995). *Escape from poverty: What makes a difference?* New York: Cambridge University Press.

Conger, R. D., Jewsbury-Conger, K., & Elder, G.H. (1997). Family and economic hardship and adolescent adjustment: Mediating and moderating processes. In G. J. Duncan & J. Brooks-Gunn (Eds.), *Consequences of growing up poor* (pp. 288-310). New York: Russell Sage Foundation.

Council on Scientific Affairs. (January 9, 1991). Hispanic health in the United States. *Journal of the American Medical Association, 265*(2), 248-252.

Danziger, S. (1989). Fighting poverty and reducing welfare dependency. In P.H. Cottingham & D. T. Ellwood (Eds.), *Welfare policy for the 1990s* (pp. 41-69). Cambridge, MA: Harvard University Press.

Darby, M. R. (1996). Facing and reducing poverty. In M.R. Darby (Ed.), *Reducing poverty in America: Views and approaches* (pp. 3-12). Thousand Oaks, CA: Sage Publications.

De La Rosa, M. (1998). Prevalence and consequences of alcohol, cigarette, and drug abuse among Hispanics. *Alcoholism Quarterly Treatment, 16*, 21-55.

De La Rosa, M. (1989). Hispanics and health and the responsiveness of the health care system. *Health and Social Work, 14*(2), 104-113.

Delgado, M. (1977). Puerto Rican spiritualism and the social work profession. *Social Casework, 58*(2), 451-458.

Duncan, G. J., & Brooks-Gunn, J. (1997). *Consequences of growing up poor.* New York: Russell Sage Foundation.

Elder, J. P., Castro, F. G., Moor, C., Mayer, J., Candelaria, J. I., Campbell, N., Talavera, G., & Ware, L. M. (1991). Differences in cancer-risk-related behaviors in Latino and Anglos. *Preventive Medicine, 20*, 751-763.

Federal Register (February 28, 1998). Volume 63(36), 9235-9238.

Fitzgerald, H. E., Lester, B. M., & Zuckerman, B. (1995). *Children of poverty: Research, health, and policy.* New York: Garland Publishing, Inc.

Fitzpatrick, J. P. (1987). *Puerto Ricans Americans: The meaning of migration to the mainland.* Englewood Cliffs, NY: Prentice Hall.

Garcia-Coll, C., & Vasquez Garcia, H. A. (1995). Hispanic children and their families: On a different track from the beginning. In H. E. Fitzgerald, B. M. Lester, & B. Zuckerman (Eds.), *Children of poverty: Research, health, and policy* (pp. 57-78). New York: Garland Publishing.

Ginsberg, L. (1996). *Understanding social problems, policies, and programs.* Columbia. SC: University of South Carolina Press.

Ginzberg, E. (January 9, 1991). Access to health care for Hispanics. *Journal of the American Medical Association, 265*(2), 238-241.

Harwood, A. (1977). *Spiritist as needed: A study of a Puerto Rican community mental health resource.* New Jersey: Prentice-Hall.

Harrington, M. (1984). *The new American poverty.* New York: Penguin Books.

Huston, A. (1991). *Children in poverty: Child development and public policy.* Cambridge, MA: Cambridge, University Press.

Johnston, L. D., O'Malley, P. M., and Bachman, J. G. (In Press). *National survey results on drug use from the monitoring the future study, 1975-1997.* (NIH Publication. No. 96-4139). Vol. I. Rockville, MD.

Kelso, W. (1994). *Poverty and the underclass: Changing perceptions of the poor in America.* New York: New York University Press.

Kumanyika, S., Savage, D. D., & Ramirez, A. G. (1989). Beliefs about high blood pressure prevention in a survey of blacks and Hispanics. *American Journal of Preventive Medicine, 5,* 21-26.

Landes, D. S. (1998). *The wealth and poverty of nations: Why some are rich and some so poor.* New York: W. W. Norton & Company.

Lieberson, S., & Waters, M. C. (1987). The location of ethnic and racial groups in the United States. *Sociological Forum 2,* 780-810.

McMillen, M., Kaufman, P., & Klein, S. (1997). *Dropout rates in the United States: 1995.* Washington, D.C.: U.S. Department of Education, National Center for Education Statistics.

Munoz, E., Lecca, P. J., & Goldstein, J. D. (1988). *A profile of Puerto Rican health in the United States: Data from the Hispanic Health and Nutrition Examination Survey, 1982-84.* New York: Long Island Medical Center.

National Council of La Raza. (1990). *Twenty-Two Hispanic leaders discuss poverty.* Washington, D.C.: National Councila of La Raza.

National Council of La Raza. (1997). *Welfare to work issue brief.* Washington, D.C.: National Council of La Raza.

National Council of La Raza (1995). *Testimony to U.S. Congress on the impact of welfare reform on the Hispanic community.* Washington, D.C.: National Council of La Raza.

National Research Council. (1996). *Measuring poverty: A new approach.* Washington, D.C.: National Academy of Science Press.

New York Times. (January 29, 1999). Fed chief warns of painful choices on social security, p. A1.

Perez, S. M., & De la Rosa, D. (1993). Economic, labor force and social implication of Latino educational and population trends. *Hispanic Journal of Behavioral Science, 15*(2), 188-229.

Portes, A., & Rumbaut, R. G. (1996). *Immigrant America: A portrait.* Berkeley, CA: University of California Press.

Purdum, T. (November 5, 1998). Victory shines light on shift in population. *The New York Times,* p. B2.

Roberts, E. (1997). Neighborhood social environment and the distribution of low birth weight in Chicago. *American Journal of Public Health, 87*(4), 597-603.

Sack, K. (November 6, 1998). Black turnout in the south led to surge by democrats. The *New York Times,* p. A1, A28.

Shiono, P. H., Rauh, V. A., Park, M., Lederman, S. A., & Zuskar, D. (1997). Ethnic differences in birth weights: The role of lifestyle and other factors. *American Journal of Public Health, 87* (5), 787-793.

Singer, M. (1994). AIDS and the health crisis of the U.S. urban poor: The perspective of critical medical anthropology. *Social Science Medicine*, 39(7), 931-948.

Smith, J. R., Brooks-Gunn, J., & Klebanov, P. K. (1997). Consequences of living in poverty for young children's cognitive and verbal ability and early school achievement. In G. J. Duncan & J. Brooks-Gunn (Eds.), *Consequences of growing up poor* (132-189). New York: Russell Sage Foundation.

Stern, M. (1984). *Factors relating to increased prevalence of diabetes in Hispanic Americans*. Unpublished manuscript, Task Force on Black and Minority Health, DHHS, Washington, D.C.

Strang, W., Winglee, M., & Stunkard, J. (1993). *Characteristics of secondary-school-age language minority and limited English proficient youth*. Washington, D.C: U.S. Department of Education.

Suro, R. (1998). *Strangers among us: How Latino immigration is transforming America*. New York: Alfred F. Knopf Inc.

Substance Abuse and Mental Health Services Administration. (1994a). *National household survey on drug abuse: Population estimates, October 1997*. (DHHS Pub. No. 94-3017). Washington, D.C.: U.S. Government Printing Office.

U.S. Department of Health and Human Services. (1985). *Report of the secretary's task force on black and minority health*. (DHHS Publication No. 85-487). Washington, D.C.: U.S. Government Printing Office.

U.S. Department of Commerce, Bureau of the Census. (1997a). *Projections of the Hispanic population: 1993-2080*. (Current Populations Reports Series, Supplement, March 1997). Washington, D.C.: U.S. Government Printing Office.

U.S. Department of Commerce, Bureau of the Census. (1997b). *Poverty in the United States: 1996*. (Current Populations Reports, Series P-60, No., 198). Washington, D.C.: U.S. Government Printing Office.

U.S. Department of Commerce, Bureau of the Census. (1997c). *Household relationship, race and Hispanic origin, and selected status*. (Current Populations Reports Series, Supplement, March 1997). Washington, D.C.: U.S. Government Printing Office.

U.S. Department of Commerce, Bureau of the Census. (1997d). *Hispanic population of the United States*. (Current Populations Reports Series, Supplement, March 1997). Washington, D.C.: U.S. Government Printing Office.

U.S. Department of Commerce, Bureau of the Census. (1997e). *Work experience during year by selected characteristics: Poverty status in 1996*. (Current Populations Reports Series, Supplement, March 1997). Washington, D.C.: U.S. Government Printing Office.

U.S. Department of Commerce, Bureau of the Census. (1997f). *Earning of persons by race and ethnicity: Both sexes*. (Current Populations Reports Series, Supplement, March 1997). Washington, D.C.: U.S. Government Printing Office.

U.S. Department of Commerce, Bureau of the Census. (1997g). *Selected economic characteristics of all persons and Hispanic persons by type of origin*. (Current Populations Reports Series, Supplement, March 1997). Washington, D.C.: U.S. Government Printing Office.

U.S. Department of Commerce, Bureau of the Census. (1997h). *Educational attain-*

ment in the United States. (Current Populations Reports, Series P-20). Washington, DC: U.S. Government Printing Office.

U.S. Department of Commerce, Bureau of the Census. (1997i). *Years of school completed by selected characteristics–Poverty status in 1996 of persons 25 years old or older.* (Current Populations Reports Series, Supplement, March 1997). Washington, D.C.: U.S. Government Printing Office.

U.S. Department of Commerce, Bureau of the Census. (1997j). *Dropout rates in the United States.* Washington, D.C. Unpublished Data.

U.S. Department of Labor, Bureau of Labor Statistics. (1998). *Employment status of the civilian population by race, sex, age, and Hispanic origin.* Washington, D.C.: U.S. Government Printing Office.

U.S. Department of Commerce, Bureau of the Census. (1996). *Poverty among demographic groups, selected years: 1959-1994.* Washington, D.C.: U.S. Government Printing Office.

Trevino, F. M., Moyer, E., Valdez, B., & Stroup-Benham, C. A. (January, 9, 1991). Health insurance coverage and utilization of health services by Mexican-Americans, mainland Puerto Ricans, and Cubans. *Journal of the American Medical Association, 265*(2), 233-238.

Vega, W. A., Gil, A., & Wagner, E. (1998). Cultural adjustment and Hispanic adolescents. In Vega, W. A. & Gil, A. (Eds.), *Drug use and ethnicity in early adolescents* (pp. 125-148). New York: Plenun Press.

Villar, H. V., & Menck, H. R. (1994). The national cancer data base report on cancer in Hispanics. *Cancer, 74*(8), 2386-2396.

Wilson, W. J. (1996). *When work disappears: The world of the new urban poor.* New York: Vintage Press.

Financial Barriers to Health Care for Latinos: Poverty and Beyond

Llewellyn J. Cornelius

SUMMARY. This study uses data from the 1994 Commonwealth Fund Minority Health Survey to examine the financing of medical care for working age (18-64) Latinos. Nearly one out of every three working age Latinos (32.4 percent) were uninsured in 1994. Poor Latinos were more than three times more likely than upper income Latinos (49.9 percent versus 13.8 percent) to lack health insurance in 1994. Uninsured Latinos were less likely than those with public or private insurance to see a physician in 1994 (62.7 percent versus 88.9 and 89.3 percent respectively). Multivariate analyses showed that both financial (income, employment status, amount of insurance premiums) and non-financial factors (type of usual source of medical care, citizenship) played a role in a decision to see a physician in 1994. Options are discussed for expanding coverage to the uninsured. *[Article copies available for a fee from The Haworth Document Delivery Service: 1-800-342-9678. E-mail address: <getinfo@haworthpressinc.com> Website: <http://www.haworthpressinc.com>]*

KEYWORDS. Latinos, health care, uninsured, poverty, financial barriers

Llewellyn J. Cornelius is affiliated with the University of Maryland School of Social Work.

The author would like to thank The Commonwealth Fund for their support in this analytic effort.

The information reported in this paper reflects the views of the author and no official endorsement by The Commonwealth Fund, or the University of Maryland, School of Social Work is intended or should be inferred.

[Haworth co-indexing entry note]: "Financial Barriers to Health Care for Latinos: Poverty and Beyond." Cornelius, Llewellyn J. Co-published simultaneously in *Journal of Poverty* (The Haworth Press, Inc.) Vol. 4, No. 1/2, 2000, pp. 63-83; and: *Latino Poverty in the New Century: Inequalities, Challenges and Barriers* (ed: Maria Vidal de Haymes, Keith M. Kilty, and Elizabeth A. Segal) The Haworth Press, Inc., 2000, pp. 63-83. Single or multiple copies of this article are available for a fee from The Haworth Document Delivery Service [1-800-342-9678, 9:00 a.m. - 5:00 p.m. (EST). E-mail address: getinfo@haworthpressinc.com].

Latinos represent the fastest growing ethnic population in the United States, yet they continue to encounter significant barriers to obtaining medical care. Financial barriers are seen as one of the major obstacles to Latino access to care (Schur, Albers, and Berk, 1995). However there are a multitude of other factors (immigration patterns, discrimination, prejudice, geographic mobility, etc.) that are intertwined with the ability of Latinos to obtain medical care. Thus any effort to examine the barriers to health care for Latinos requires the consideration of both financial and non-financial barriers to care.

For all Americans, the lack of private insurance and public insurance before 1965 created a significant barrier to care. Before the development of private health insurance plans during the depression, access to medical care was determined by one's ability to pay for care out-of-pocket, or the good will of charitable institutions (Starr, 1982; Anderson, 1990). The development of employment based private insurance plans during the depression, and public insurance options (most notably Medicare and Medicaid in 1965), vastly increased the proportion of Americans who had some form of health insurance. By 1953, 41% of the low income (< $3,000 in 1953) and 80% of the upper income families (> $4,999 in 1953) in America had health insurance (Anderson and Andersen, 1967). In 1963, 51% of the low-income (< $4,000 in 1963) families and 89% of the upper income families in America (> $7,000 in 1963) had health insurance (Anderson and Andersen, 1967).

While having employment based health insurance increased access to care, the ability to have insurance was not only linked to having a job, it was correlated with the type of job. Historical patterns of immigration for Latinos are closely tied to the economic situation of Latinos and hence their ability to obtain health insurance. Close to three-quarters of Latinos are either Mexican/Chicano (60 percent) or Puerto Rican (12.2 percent). Cubans comprise close to 5 percent (4.7 percent) of this group, while Central and South American Latinos comprise the remaining 22.7 percent (U.S. Department of Commerce, 1998). Bean and Tienda indicate that Mexican/Chicanos and Puerto Ricans were both primarily recruited to work in blue collar, unskilled jobs (Bean and Tienda, 1990). Mexican/Chicanos and Puerto Ricans were also the victims of intense prejudice, discrimination, subordination and economic segregation. The difference between the two was that Chicanos were initially recruited for rural agricultural jobs, while

Puerto Ricans were recruited for urban, seasonal jobs in the manufacturing or service sector. The economic situation for urban Puerto Ricans worsened in the 1970s after manufacturing jobs moved from the central city to the suburbs (Bean and Tienda, 1990, p. 26).

Cuban immigration reflected a different set of economic circumstances. The majority of early Cuban immigrants were political refugees. A large portion of these immigrants were middle and upper income urban professionals. Immigrants who arrived after the Mariel boatlift (1980) "resemble(d) traditional immigrants whose decisions to leave were governed by economic factors" (Bean and Tienda, 1990, p. 29). Over time, differences in immigration translated into economic differences between these ethnic groups. Anglo-Americans fared better than Latinos and African Americans during the 1960s and 1970s in the areas of education and employment (Jaynes and Williams, 1989; NAHP, 1996). During the same period there was also an increase in the disparity in earnings between Latinos, African Americans and Anglo-Americans (Jaynes and Williams, 1989; NAHP, 1996). In 1980, while 9.7 percent of Anglo Americans lived in poverty, 26.9 percent of Latinos lived in poverty (U.S. Congress, 1994). Close to 12 percent (11.7 percent) of Cubans were in poverty, compared with 20.6 percent of Mexican Americans, 34.9 percent of Puerto Ricans and 16.7 percent of other Latinos (Bean and Tienda, 1990).

Labor force participation rates reflect similar trends between Mexican, Puerto Rican and Cuban Americans. The labor force participation rate was the lowest for Puerto Ricans, while it was the highest for Cuban Americans (Bean and Tienda, 1990; Knouse, Rosenfield and Culbertson, 1992). By 1989 Mexican Americans and Puerto Ricans were more likely than Cuban or Anglo Americans to be employed as operators, fabricators or laborers or to be employed in service occupations. However, they were less likely than Cuban or Anglo-Americans to be employed in managerial or professional positions (Knouse, Rosenfield and Culbertson, 1992). In addition, Mexican Americans were more likely than other Latinos or Anglo-Americans to be employed in the farming, forestry and fishing industries (Knouse, Rosenfield and Culbertson, 1992). Acs (1995) found that in 1988 and 1991 the working poor, the unemployed and workers in the mining, construction, retail, manufacturing and wholesale industries were less likely to be insured. He also found that falling family incomes accounted for most of the decline of insurance between 1988 and 1991.

Acs also noticed a general decline in employer sponsored health insurance over this period (Acs, 1995). Thus Latinos are more likely to be concentrated among the working poor, a group that is less likely than others to have health insurance coverage (Short, Cornelius and Goldstone, 1990).

Latino's ability to obtain health insurance is not only tied to patterns of employment, it is also tied to the way public and private insurance programs are designed. A case in point is the Medicaid program. In the years since its enactment, Medicaid has become a critical component of the U.S. health care system and the primary national program financing health care for the poor and medically needy. It currently constitutes one of the largest single components of state budgets, with expenditures totaling $125 billion (57% federal and 43% state) for medical services to more than 25 million individuals in federal fiscal year 1993 (Liska, Obermaier, Lyons and Long, 1995).

While the Medicaid program was enacted in 1965 to encourage states to increase the provision of medical care to the poor, it was built on the then existing federally supported welfare programs for families with dependent children, thus limiting the eligibility to the poor covered under those programs. Aside from covering a subset of the poor, Medicaid eligibility was extended primarily to the aged, blind, and disabled. Also included were individuals whose income was too high to make them eligible for a cash payment, but who had high medical expenses relative to income and met the non-financial eligibility, called categorical, criteria for welfare. These people were called the "medically needy." There have been some recent eligibility expansions of the program, but for the most part the program remains limited to certain categories of the poor (Iglehart, 1993). Recent expansions included mandates to cover women and children with incomes below the poverty line, and low income pregnant women (Iglehart, 1993). Recent restrictions (following the enactment of P.L. 104-193–the Personal Responsibility and Work Opportunities Act of 1996) include: a re-definition of a childhood disability (thus reducing the number of children with disabilities covered by Medicaid); and an exclusion of certain classes of documented and undocumented poor immigrants from Medicaid coverage (Health Care Financing Administration 1998a, 1998b).

As of 1997, Medicaid provided health care coverage to more than 33.5 million Americans (Health Care Financing Administration,

1998c). Nearly half (15.2 million) of these beneficiaries are children (Health Care Financing Administration, 1998c). Medicaid also provided coverage for services provided to 3.9 million elderly, 6.1 million blind and disabled persons and 6.7 million low income adults, including pregnant women (Health Care Financing Administration, 1998c). For the groups targeted by the Medicaid program, the availability of Medicaid has led to increases of the chances of being seeing by a physician, improvement in prenatal care and improvements in health status (Davis, 1979)

Despite its commitment to providing care for the indigent, most critics contend that the Medicaid program is seriously flawed. First, Medicaid expenditures have more than doubled since 1989 (Iglehart, 1993). As a result Medicaid has become a prime target for cost containment programs, cutbacks in programs for the poor, attempts to increase general state taxes, or attempts to cut back other state programs (Coughlin, Ku, Holahan, Hesiam, and Winterbottom, 1994). Second, although Medicaid was designed to provide access to care for the poor, most estimates place the proportion of the noninstitutionalized poor covered by the program at less than 50 percent. Third, less than half of the participating Medicaid physicians accept all patients (Perloff, Kletke and Fossett, 1995). Fourth, the majority (59 percent) of health care expenditures for Medicaid are for the disabled, the blind and the aged, who constitute only 27 percent of the Medicaid enrollees (Liska, Obermaier, Lyons and Long, 1995). Finally, because the program is administered at the state level and only limited data are collected by the federal government, it has been difficult to estimate on a national basis the proportion of the near poor, aged, the disabled, minorities and other groups who are targets of the Medicaid program. However, it is believed that the inability of Medicaid to cover all of the poor creates a gap in coverage for poor Latinos.

Like Medicaid, private health insurance in the United States was at best a partial solution to the more global problem of the lack of universal health insurance. While the provision of some form of universal health insurance has been achieved by other countries (e.g., Canada, England, Denmark (Raffel, 1984)), it has long been an elusive goal in the U.S. Universal health insurance has not been adopted in the U.S. because it has been opposed by various factions since the beginning of the century. Since the depression, though, several private insurance options were developed to make health care affordable for most Americans. Starting with the "fee for service" plans at Baylor University in 1929 and the development of the Kaiser Permanente and the Health Insurance Plan of New York as "Health Maintenance Organizations" in the 1940s (Starr, 1982; Anderson, 1990), private insurance became the pillar of the health insurance system in the United States. Until the 1980s, Health Maintenance Organizations (managed care, coordinated care, or capitated payments systems) covered only a small portion of the U.S. population. Recently, though, the spiraling cost of health expenditures has fostered the exponential growth of managed care programs as a cost containment strategy. Along with the evolution of managed care organizations, other cost containment strategies have evolved, including: the elimination of health insurance as a fringe benefit (as an employer cost savings strategy), the restriction of the scope of health coverage, and an increase in out-of-pocket costs for those with health coverage. Like public insurance, the lack of access to private insurance coverage has led to some Latinos falling in between the cracks.

Current health care financing arrangements tend to underserve African and Latino Americans, the poor, the unemployed, the employed who work in industries without health coverage and low wage workers (Short, Monheit and Beauregard, 1989; Short, Cornelius and Goldstone, 1990). In 1987 over three-quarters (77 percent) of uninsured Latinos were in families with at least one adult worker (Short, Cornelius and Goldstone, 1990). Fifty-one percent of these uninsured Latinos lived in poverty (Short, Cornelius and Goldstone, 1990). During the same year, 18.5 percent of Mexican Americans, 13.1 percent of Puerto Ricans and 20.0 percent of Cubans were uninsured some time during the year (Schur, Bernstein and Berk, 1987). Between 1977 and 1996 the number of uninsured Latinos increased from two to nine million (Short, Cornelius and Goldstone, 1990; Vistnes and Monheit, 1997). During the same time period it increased from four to seven million for African Americans and from 18 to 24 million for Anglo-Americans (Short, Cornelius and Goldstone, 1990; Vistnes and Monheit, 1997).

The availability of insurance is an important factor to consider in examining access to health care because of the effects of being uninsured. One study found that the uninsured were less likely than those with insurance to be able to obtain emergency care, to be hospitalized, to obtain pediatric care, mental health care, prescribed medicines, home health care, medical equipment or medical supplies (Himmelstein and Woodhandler, 1995). Uninsured patients and patients with Medicaid faced a higher risk of a ruptured appendix than persons with private coverage (Braveman, Schaaf, Egerter, Benet and Schecter, 1994). The mortality rates for those without health insurance was three times higher than for persons with insurance (Hadley, Steinberg and Feder, 1991). Franks and colleagues reported that the long-term lack of insurance coverage increased the rate of premature death among Americans (Franks, Clancy and Gold, 1993).

These findings suggest that financial factors can pose a significant barrier to care for Latinos. There may also be other factors that influence one's ability to obtain needed medical services. The purpose of this paper is twofold: first, to use recent data to examine how working age (ages 18-64) Latino Americans fare on correlates of the financing of care (insurance, income, and insurance premiums); and second, to examine the factors that facilitate the use of physician services for working age Latinos with private insurance, public insurance and the uninsured. Data from the 1994 Commonwealth Fund Minority Health Survey will be used to address these issues.

DATA AND METHODS

The data used in this paper are from the 1994 Commonwealth Fund Minority Health Survey, conducted by Lou Harris and Associates (1994) for The Commonwealth Fund. A national probability sample of approximately 3,789 adults 18 years of age and older was selected for this survey. This study focused on a subpopulation of Latinos between the ages of 18 and 64 (n = 942). This survey used a national probability sample of telephone households in the 48 contiguous United States (excluding Alaska and Hawaii). The telephone sample employed random digit selection procedures that assured equal representation of persons in both households that are "listed" in telephone directories, and persons in households that are "unlisted." Besides the random cross-section sample, oversamples of African Americans and Hispanics were obtained by screening additional national cross sections and interviewing only African Americans and Hispanics until the desired sample sizes had been achieved. Finally, interviews were conducted with Asian Americans included in list samples (based on surnames listed in telephone directories) provided by Survey Sampling

Inc. The findings reported by the sampled respondent were weighted to reflect their proportionate representation of the U.S. population as reflected in the Bureau of the Census March 1994 Current Population Survey. These weights account for the differences that occur in the probability of selecting an individual from the population.

RACE AND ETHNICITY

Classification by ethnic/racial background was based on information reported for each household member. Respondents were asked if their racial background was best described as African American, Black, Asian or Pacific Islander, Native American or Alaskan Native, White or another race. All respondents were also asked whether their main national origin or ancestry was among the following Hispanic-American subpopulations, regardless of racial background: Puerto Rican, Cuban, Mexican, Dominican, Costa Rican, Colombian, Ecuadorian, Honduran, El Salvadoran or other Hispanic. The respondents who stated they were African American were also asked if they were of Caribbean heritage. The respondents who indicated they were Asian or Pacific Islanders were also asked if they were either Chinese, Vietnamese, Korean or of some other Asian heritage. The categories of Anglo-American, and African American were formed by taking only those whites, blacks, and African Americans who were not Hispanic (Latino) and placing them into their respective groups. The terms "Hispanics," "Latinos" and "Latino Americans" are used interchangeably in this paper to describe the experiences of those identified as Hispanics in the survey.

INSURANCE

Insurance data presented in this paper were based on self-reported data from the survey respondents. Questions were asked to determine whether a person was covered on the interview date by health insurance through work or union; health insurance through someone else's work or union; health insurance purchased directly by the respondent or his/her family, some other group insurance, Medicare, or Medicaid. The category "Private Insurance Only" represented persons who had either health insurance through work or union, health insurance purchased directly by the respondent or his/her family or some other group insurance but did not have Medicare, Medicaid or some other public insurance. The category "Any Public Insurance" represented persons who had either Medicaid or Medicare on the date of the interview, regardless of whether they have some form of private insurance. The category "uninsured" represented the persons who did not fall into any of the above insurance categories.

MEASURE OF DISCRIMINATION

Questions regarding discrimination experienced by the respondent were based on self-reports of mistreatment or discrimination. The variable "any discrimination" represented persons who reported having health care experiences in the previous 12 months where they were mistreated. It also includes persons who felt they would have received better care if they belonged to a different race or ethnic group or persons who felt they were treated badly because of race/ethnicity, sex, age, health or disability, income level or any other reason.

TESTS OF SIGNIFICANCE

Tests of significance were conducted (using a statistical package called SUDAAN (Shah, Barnwell, Hunt, LaVange, 1992) to determine the statistical significance of the findings presented in this paper. Two tests of statistical significance were used to detect whether the data reported in these analyses were statistically significant. The first statistic used was the standard error. A major purpose of the 1994 Commonwealth Fund Survey is to allow for the construction of population estimates based on sample data. Like all probability samples, there is a margin of error between the response given by a sampled respondent and what the actual response to a question would be if a census was taken. The "standard error" represents the difference between the reported results and what the results would have been if a census of the total population was taken. Percents displayed in tables and figures with a relative standard error of more than 30 percent are noted in the tables with an asterisk. This indicates that the actual response by the population for a given question may be at least 30 percent higher or lower than what is listed in the table.

The second statistic used to perform tests of statistical significance in this study is the Student T test. The Student's T test was used to determine the statistical significance of two percents or means being compared in the analysis and to test the significance of the coefficients reported in the regression analyses. Unless otherwise noted, only statistically significant differences (p < .05) are discussed in the text.

DESCRIPTIVE FINDINGS

One out of every three (32.3 percent) working age Latino adults were uninsured in 1994 (Table 1). Slightly over 9 percent (9.4 percent) had either Medicaid, Medicare or some other public insurance, while 58.3 percent had private insurance. Although not reported in the

TABLE 1. Insurance coverage for Latinos by ethnic background, income and employment status, 1994 (ages 18-64).

	Insurance Status		
Characteristic	Private Only	Any Public Insurance	Uninsured
Total	58.3%	9.4%	32.3%
Ethnic Background			
Mexican/Chicano	60.5%	8.3%	31.2%
Puerto Ricans	57.7%	16.4%	25.9%
Other Latinos	53.2%	5.9%	40.9%
Income			
< 15,001	27.2%	22.9%	49.9%
15,001-25,000	46.4%	8.3%	45.3%
25,001-50,000	73.6%	3.0%	23.5%
50,001+	80.0%	6.2%	13.8%
Employment Status			
Full time	70.7%	4.3%	25.0%
Part time	39.6%	5.5%	54.9%
Not in the labor force	31.3%	21.7%	47.0%
Unemployed	45.5%	24.5%*	30.0%

Note: * Standard error of a percent ≥ 30 percent

Source: The Commonwealth Fund, 1994

tables, uninsured Latinos were less likely than persons with public insurance or private insurance to see a physician in 1994 (62.7 percent versus 88.9 percent and 89.2 percent respectively (p < .01)).

Latinos from the Dominican Republic, Costa Rica, Colombia, Equador, El Salvador or the Honduras, poor Latinos and near poor Latinos, part time Latino workers and Latino workers who were not in the labor force were disproportionately represented among the uninsured. Nearly a quarter (25.9 percent) of the Puerto Ricans were uninsured compared with 31.2 percent of the Mexican/Chicano Americans and 40.0 percent of the other Latinos (p < .001). Poor Latinos were over three times more likely than upper income Latinos (49.9 percent versus 13.8 percent) to lack health insurance in 1994 (p < .001). Finally, part time Latino workers and Latinos who were not in the labor force were more likely than full time workers to be uninsured in 1994 (p < .01).

About one out of every ten (9.4 percent) working age Latinos spent more than $200 per month in insurance premiums in 1994 (Table 2). Upper income Latinos are disproportionately represented in this group. Less than 9 percent of the Puerto Ricans and Mexicans were in this group, compared with 18.9 percent of other Latinos (p < .01). In addition, over 13 percent of the upper income Latinos (13.5 percent) spent more than $200 per month in insurance premiums, compared to 2.5 percent of the lowest income group (p < .001).

The disparities by income and employment status on insurance and monthly premiums appear even larger when one examines ethnic differences within these categories (Tables 3-4). For example, low income Mexican Americans were even more disadvantaged than other Mexican Americans when it came to the issue of health coverage. Over half of the low income Mexican Americans lack health insurance coverage, while 10.9 percent of the upper income Mexican Americans were without coverage in 1994 (p < .001) (Table 3). Likewise over 60 percent (60.8 percent) of the low income Latinos from the Dominican Republic, Costa Rica, Colombia, Equador, El Salvador or the Honduras were without health insurance, compared with 23.7 percent of the higher income Latinos from the Dominican Republic, Costa Rica, Colombia, Equador, El Salvador or the Honduras (p < .001). Next, Puerto Ricans who were not in the labor force were twice as likely as Puerto Ricans who were full time workers to lack health insurance in 1994 (51.6 percent vs. 19.9 percent) (p < .01). Finally, middle income

TABLE 2. Monthly insurance premiums for Latinos by ethnic background, income and employment status (ages 18-64), 1994.

Characteristic	Monthly Insurance Premiums				
	None	$1-49	$50-99	$100-199	$200+
Total	31.1%	25.5%	16.6%	17.4%	9.4%
Ethnic Background					
Mexican/Chicano	28.7%	24.9%	19.1%	19.3%	8.1%
Puerto Ricans	40.1%	33.3%	12.4%	9.2%	5.0%
Other Latinos	31.9%	20.5%	10.2%	18.5%	18.9%
Income					
< 15,001	48.8%	20.5%	17.6%	10.7%*	2.5%*
15,001-25,000	26.2%	30.4%	13.3%	19.1%	11.0%
25,001-50,000	25.9%	27.4%	16.7%	20.9%	9.1%
50,001+	30.6%	22.6%	18.0%	15.4%	13.5%
Employment Status					
Full time	26.3%	26.8%	18.8%	18.3%	9.8%
Part time	22.6%	36.0%*	15.3%*	17.2%*	8.9%*
Not in the labor force	42.8%	14.7%	13.8%*	20.4%	8.3%
Unemployed	54.2%	20.1%	7.1%	10.3%	8.3%*

Note: * Standard error of a percent ≥ 30 percent

Source: The Commonwealth Fund, 1994

Puerto Ricans were five times more likely than low income Puerto Ricans to pay between $1 and $49 per month for health insurance premiums.

MULTIVARIATE FINDINGS

Displayed in Table 5 are correlates of the probability of seeing a physician in 1994 by insurance status. The findings indicate that socioeconomic factors played a significant role in the decision to see a physician for those with private insurance, but not for those with public insurance or the uninsured.

For Latinos with private insurance, the amount of the insurance premium, income, employment status, perceived health status, perceptions of discrimination, region of residence, the type of usual source of care and gender were correlated with the decision to see a provider.

TABLE 3. Insurance coverage for Latinos by ethnic background, income and employment status, 1994 (ages 18-64).

Characteristic	Private Only	Any public Insurance	Uninsured
Income < $15,000			
Mexican/Chicano	28.7%	18.2%	53.1%
Puerto Ricans	18.7%	39.3%	42.0%
Other Latinos	40.9%	18.8%	40.3%
Income $15,001-25,000			
Mexican/Chicano	52.3%	7.9%	39.7%
Puerto Ricans	46.6%	15.1%*	38.3%
Other Latinos	35.2%	4.2%	60.6%
Income $25,001-50,000			
Mexican/Chicano	73.7%	2.9%	23.4%*
Puerto Ricans	85.8%	1.4%	12.8%
Other Latinos	56.4%	4.0%	39.6%
Income $50,000+			
Mexican/Chicano	82.2%	6.9%	10.9%
Puerto Ricans	76.1%	12.5%	11.4%*
Other Latinos	76.3%	.0%	23.7%
Full Time			
Mexican/Chicano	72.3%	5.8%	21.9%
Puerto Ricans	76.3%	3.8%	19.9%
Other Latinos	58.8%	1.2%	40.0%
Part Time			
Mexican/Chicano	41.9%	5.2%	52.9%
Puerto Ricans	35.8%	9.9%	54.4%
Other Latinos	44.4%	.0%	55.6%
Not in the Labor Force			
Mexican/Chicano	44.0%	19.8%	36.2%
Puerto Ricans	16.0%	32.4%	51.6%
Other Latinos	19.5%	20.8%	59.7%
Unemployed			
Mexican/Chicano	40.5%	14.8%	44.7%
Puerto Ricans	34.4%	55.7%	9.9%
Other Latinos	82.6%	7.3%	10.2%

Note: * Standard error ≥ 30 percent

Source: The Commonwealth Fund, 1994

Unemployed Latinos with private insurance were less likely than others to initiate a visit to a doctor in 1994 (p < .05). Low income Latinos with private insurance were less likely than others to see a physician in 1994 (p < .05). Latinos with private insurance who had monthly insurance premiums between $1 and $49 were more likely than other

TABLE 4. Monthly insurance premiums by income and employment status, controlling for ethnic background (ages 18-64), 1994.

Characteristic	Insurance Premiums				
	None	$1-49	$50-99	$100-199	$200+
Income < 15,001					
Mexican/Chicano	36.7%	25.7%	20.1%	13.1%	4.4%
Puerto Ricans	79.6%	9.8%	3.9%	6.7%	.0%
Other Latinos	63.8%	24.2%	12.1%	.0%	.0%
Income 15,001-25,000					
Mexican/Chicano	29.4%	27.4%	19.1%	17.5%	6.7%
Puerto Ricans	27.9%	30.8%	11.4%	22.1%	7.9%
Other Latinos	21.1%	29.4%	.0%	15.0%	34.6%
Income $25,001-50,000					
Mexican/Chicano	27.9%	22.0%	17.2%	23.0%	9.8%
Puerto Ricans	22.6%	51.4%	19.5%	2.1%	4.4%
Other Latinos	22.0%	23.1%	4.0%	39.9%	11.1%
Income $50,001+					
Mexican/Chicano	23.6%	27.8%	21.9%	18.3%	8.4%
Puerto Ricans	49.8%	24.3%	8.6%	10.3%	7.0%
Other Latinos	29.9%	10.8%	21.0%	9.4%	28.9%
Employed Full Time					
Mexican/Chicano	28.2%	23.9%	20.5%	18.4%	9.1%
Puerto Ricans	25.3%	40.1%	16.8%	10.2%	7.6%
Other Latinos	21.7%	23.5%	10.8%	26.5%	17.6%
Employed Part Time					
Mexican/Chicano	13.6%	20.0%	26.1%	29.4%	10.9%
Puerto Ricans	27.2%	72.8%	.0%	.0%	.0%
Other Latinos	45.1%	32.3%	.0%	.0%	22.6%
Not in Labor Force					
Mexican/Chicano	36.8%	26.0%	12.5%	19.6%	5.1%
Puerto Ricans	60.2%	.0%	.0%	39.8%	.0%
Other Latinos	76.6%	.0%	23.4%	.0%	.0%
Unemployed					
Mexican/Chicano	37.9%	36.1%	8.1%	17.9%	.0%
Puerto Ricans	86.3%	4.6%	6.5%	2.6%	.0%
Other Latinos	24.6%	23.0%	.0%	12.6%	39.9%

Note: * Standard error ≥ 30 percent

Source: The Commonwealth Fund, 1994

Latinos to see a physician in 1994 ($p < .05$). Latinos with private insurance who regularly used a physician's office were more likely than Latinos who had other usual sources of care to see a physician during 1994 ($p < .01$). Females with private insurance were more likely than males with private insurance to see a physician ($p < .01$).

For Latinos with public insurance only the place of birth (U.S.

TABLE 5. Probability of a physician visit (ages 18-64), 1994 (log-odds).

Characteristic	Private Insurance Only	Any Public Insurance	Uninsured
Birthplace			
Born outside of U.S.	0.73	0.07*	1.16
Ethnic Background			
Mexican/Chicano	0.58	1.42	1.00
Puerto Rican	0.75	4.63	0.92
Insurance Premiums			
$1-49	2.51*	–	–
$50-99	1.23	–	–
$100-199	0.99	–	–
$200+	0.61	–	–
Income			
< $15,000	0.69*	1.68	1.24
$15,000-25,000	1.19	2.63	0.91
$25,001-50,000	1.12	4.51	5.63
Employment Status			
Part time	0.43	6.08	1.45
Not in labor force	0.97	1.22	1.58
Unemployed	0.38*	9.55	1.20
Education Level			
< High school	0.55	0.33	1.16
High school grad	0.61	0.37	0.89
Usual Source of Care			
Doctor's Office	3.29**	3.05	1.71*
HMO	0.38	0.19	11.64
Hospital OPD	1.14	12.84	1.30
Hospital ER	0.60	1.56	1.77
Perceived Health			
Fair/Poor	4.21***	5.77	1.73
Any Discrimination	4.63**	0.13	1.72
Gender			
Female	2.83**	2.42	1.44
Age			
18-24	1.58	0.33	1.40
25-50	0.76	0.28*	0.83
Region			
North East	0.69	0.21	0.99
Mid West	5.13	0.07	0.81
South	0.39***	0.28	0.75
Residence			
Urban	0.82	0.51	1.09
Rural	0.73	1.67	0.62
X^2	18.80	11.98	16.10
df	29	25	25
N	649	110	183

Note: Excluded categories are: born in the USA, other Latinos, no monthly premiums, no out-of-pocket costs, income > $50,001, employed full time, at least a college education, other sources of care, good/excellent health, no reported discrimination, males, ages 51-64, west, suburban residents

* $p < .05$, ** $p < .01$, *** $p < .001$

Source: The Commonwealth Fund, 1994

versus non U.S. born) and age were significantly correlated with the decision to see a physician in 1994. Latinos with public insurance who were born outside of the U.S. were less likely than other Latinos with public insurance to see a physician in 1994 ($p < .05$). At the same time Latinos with public insurance between the ages of 25 and 50 were less likely than other Latinos with public insurance to initiate a physician visit in 1994 ($p < .05$).

Neither ethnic background, nor social economic factors played a significant role in whether or not uninsured Latinos would initiate a visit to a physician. In fact the other significant correlate of the use of medical services for uninsured Latinos was their type of usual source of care. Uninsured Latinos with a physician's office as their usual source of care were more likely than other uninsured Latinos to see a doctor in 1994.

CONCLUSIONS AND IMPLICATIONS

This study indicates that in 1994, close to one third (32.3 percent) of all working age Latinos were uninsured. By contrast in 1977, one in five (20.0 percent) of all working age Latinos were uninsured (Short, Cornelius and Goldstone, 1990). Income and employment status was correlated with the decision of Latinos with private insurance to see a physician. The cost of the private insurance premium was also correlated with the decision to see a physician for Latinos with private insurance.

Along with demonstrating that there were gaps in insurance coverage by economic factors, this study also concluded that non economic factors played a major role in the decision of Latinos to seek medical care. Foreign born Latinos with public insurance were less likely than other Latinos to see a physician in 1994. Persons with private insurance who perceived they were victims of discrimination were more likely than others to see a physician in 1994.

These findings have several implications. First, the reluctance of foreign born Latinos with public insurance to seek medical care ties into current and historical trends in the mistreatment of Latinos, the most notable of which was the passage of proposition 187 in 1994 in California. Proposition 187 prohibits state and local government from providing publicly funded education, health care, welfare and social services to anyone they do not verify either as a U.S. citizen or a documented resident of the United States. Evidence of the impact of proposition 187 is already emerging. The passage of proposition 187 in California led to a decrease in the use of mental health services by Latinos in California (Fenton, Caralano, and Hargreaves, 1996). In addition, close to half of the clinic directors in a sample of California clinics serving low income groups thought that the number of client visits by Latinos declined after the passage of proposition 187 (Fenton, Moss, Khalil, and Asch, 1997). Finally, a survey of Latina immigrants found that they saw proposition 187 as discriminatory and directed at Latinos, "building on existing fears about their economically and socially marginalized position" (Moss, Baumeister, and Biewener, 1996). The current mistreatment of Latino immigrants in the southwest appears to be part of a historical trend. Bean and Teinda suggest that there has been a cyclical pattern of immigration of Mexican workers during the twentieth century, "with the doors open in times of labor shortages, followed by restrictive policies and even massive deportations during periods of economic recession" (Bean and Tienda, 1990). Even after they arrived in the U.S., they were often victims of economic oppression and discrimination (Gann and Duignan, 1986). These findings reinforce the notion that policies directed against Latinos may have a detrimental effect on their access to medical care.

A second implication that evolves from the findings of this study is that socio-economic differences for Latinos with private insurance may lead to major barriers to health care for working poor Latinos. It was indicated earlier that the majority of uninsured Latinos were in families with at least one working adult. They were also more likely to be employed in industries that do not provide private insurance coverage. These persons may fall in between the cracks because they are not eligible for public insurance and may contribute to the growing number of uninsured Latinos. In the face of the knowledge that the numbers of uninsured are increasing, policy makers, and health care organizations continue to argue over who will pay for the coverage. While the current debate over expanding coverage to the uninsured may be seen by some as a recent crisis in the health system, the evolving debate is old indeed. Historical discussions of health insurance in America (Starr, 1982; Anderson, 1990) have indicated that the evolution of health care coverage has been piecemeal and more responsive to political contingencies than to the moral issue of whether or not health insurance should be a right or a privilege.

Given the continued lack of improvement in access to care for some Latinos and other Americans and the continued gaps in insurance coverage, the problem of the growing number of uninsured in America will not be resolved without a fundamental decision to accept and assert the idea of health coverage as a right for all Americans, not just a privilege for those who can afford it. This will require that all Americans, especially the disadvantaged, advocate for the provision of some minimum level of health coverage. From a public policy point of view this idea may only work if it is not tied to employment, or a needs based social welfare program. Keeping health insurance tied to employment will not work in the long term because employers can simply reduce or eliminate health insurance as a fringe benefit. This would lead to an increase, not a decrease, in the number of uninsured Latinos. Keeping health insurance tied to categorical social welfare programs will not work in the long haul, because of the stigma that would be attached to the program and because it may foster a dependency on that social program.

Two important changes are needed to foster making health insurance a right for all Americans: (1) A need to promote a broad based belief by all Americans that health insurance coverage is a fundamental right that should be guaranteed by virtue of being an American (which by default would make the provision of health coverage a critical responsibility of the government); and (2) The serious consideration of a more broad based tax to pay for health insurance for all Americans, such as a value added tax (VAT) on all nonessential goods and services (that is, excluding necessities–food, clothing, housing and medical care). A value added tax (VAT) is a tax on what society consumes (Rifkin, 1995). In this case society does not levy a tax on what it costs to produce a product, rather it levies a tax on the difference between what it costs a firm to produce a product and the final product itself. By excluding essential goods and services from the tax, one eliminates most of the regressive nature of the tax (Rifkin, 1995). While the VAT has not been tried in the United States, it is currently in use in more than 59 foreign countries, including most of Europe (Rifkin, 1995). Other examples of taxes that could be used for such an effort include a gasoline tax, an additional tax on social security, or a tax on tobacco or alcohol use. The problem with these approaches is that they would be targeted to a subset of Americans who may feel they are unfairly penalized (e.g., gasoline users, tobacco users). A second problem is that they would require an additional levy on taxes already being collected from the same source. In the end, the assertion of health care as a right for all is needed in order to move the debate closer to the persons who would be affected by it. It may be that we have failed to guarantee health coverage for all Americans because we have failed to convince Americans how important it is to have health coverage. The need to assert the promotion of a broad based tax is important because it would help promote the notion of health insurance as a form of social insurance. It is well known that Americans have a higher affinity for social welfare programs that are seen as social insurance entitlements (e.g., social security or unemployment insurance) as opposed to income or need based (for example Temporary Assistance for Needy Families (TANF)). Thus Americans would be more likely to approve of guaranteed health insurance if they believe that as a result of contributing to the economy, the government provides health coverage for them.

REFERENCES

Acs, G. (1995). Explaining trends in health insurance coverage between 1988 and 1991. *Inquiry, 31*: 102-10.

Aday, L.A., Andersen, R.M., Fleming, G.V. (1980). *Health Care in the U.S. Equitable for Whom?* Beverly Hills, CA: Sage Publications.

Aday, L.A., Fleming, G.V., Andersen, R.M. (1984). *Access to Medical Care: Who Has it, Who Doesn't.* Chicago, IL: Pluribus Press.

Andersen, R.M., Anderson, O.W. (1967). *A Decade of Health Services.* Chicago, IL: The University of Chicago Press.

Andersen, R.M, Lion, J., Anderson, O.W. (1975). *Two Decades of Health Services: Social Survey Trends in Use and Expenditures.* Cambridge, MA: Balinger Publishing.

Andersen, R.M., Aday, L.A., Lyttle, C.S., Cornelius, L.J., Chen, M.S. (1987). *Ambulatory Care and Insurance Coverage in an Era of Constraint.* Chicago, IL: Pluribus Press.

Andersen, O.W. (1990). *Health Services As a Growth Enterprise in the United States Since 1875.* Ann Arbor, MI: Health Administration Press.

Bean, F.D., Tienda, M. (1990). *The Hispanic population in the United States.* New York, NY: The Russell Sage Foundation.

Berk, M.L., Albers, L.A., Schur, C.L. (1996). The growth in the U.S. uninsured population: Trends in Hispanic subgroups. *American Journal of Public Health, 86*, 572-576

Braveman, P., Schaaf, V.M., Egerter, S., Bennett, T., Schecter, W. (1994). Insurance related differences in the risk of ruptured appendix. *New England Journal of Medicine, 331*: 444-9.

Coughlin, T.A., Ku, L., Holahan, J., Hesiam, D., Winterbottom, C. (1994). State Responses to the Medicaid Spending Crisis: 1988 to 1991. *Journal of Health Politics, Policy and Law 19*:837-864.

Davis, K. 1979. "Achievements and Problems of Medicaid." In Allan D. Speigel (Ed). *The Medicaid Experience.* Germantown, MD: Aspen Systems Corp.

Feldstein, P.J. (1983) *Health Care Economics* (2nd Edition). New York, NY: John Wiley and Sons.

Fenton, J.J., Caralano, R., Hargreaves, W.A. (1996). Effect of proposition 187 on mental health service in California: A Case Study. *Health Affairs, 15*: 182-90.

Fenton, J.J., Moss, N., Khalil, H.G., Asch, S. (1997). Effect of California's proposition 187 on the use of primary care clinics. *Western Journal of Medicine, 166*: 16-20.

Franks, P., Clancy, C.M., and Gold, M.R. (1993). Health Insurance and Mortality: Evidence from a National Cohort. *JAMA 270*: 737-41.

Gann, L.H., Duignan, P.J. (1986). *The Hispanics in the United States: A history.* London, England: Westview Press.

Hadley, J., Steinberg, E.P., Feder, J. (1991). Comparison of uninsured and privately insured hospital patients: Condition on admission, resource use, and outcome. *JAMA, 265*: 374-9.

Hadley, J. and Zuckerman, S. (1994). Health Reform: The good, the bad, and the bottom line. *Health Affairs 13*: 115-131.

Health Care Financing Administration (1998a). Link between Medicaid and SSI coverage of children under welfare reform. Available: http://www.hcfa.gov/medicaid/wrfs2.htm.

Health Care Financing Administration (1998b). Link between Medicaid and the immigration provisions of the personal responsibility and work opportunity act of 1996. Available: http://www.hcfa.gov/medicaid/wrfs2.htm.

Health Care Financing Administration (1998c). Medicaid Recipient by basis of eligibility and by state, fiscal year 1997. *Medicaid Program Statistics* (2082 Report). Available: http://www.hcfa.gov/medicaid/MCD97T02.htm.

Himmelstein, D.U., Woodhandler, S. (1995). Care denied: U.S. residents who are unable to obtain needed medical services. *American Journal of Public Health*, 85: 341-344.

Iglehart, J.K. (1993). The American Health Care System: Medicaid. *New England Journal of Medicine, 328*: 896-900.

Jaynes, G.D., Williams Jr., R.M. (Eds). (1989). *A Common Destiny: Blacks and American Society.* Washington, DC: National Academy Press.

Knouse, S.B., Rosenfield, P., Culbertson, A.L. (Eds). (1992) *Hispanics in the workplace.* Newbury Park, CA: Sage publications.

Loether, H.J., McTavish, D.G. (1980). *Descriptive and Inferential Statistics: An Introduction* (2nd Edition). Boston, MA: Allyn and Bacon.

Liska, D., Obermaier, K., Lyons, B., Long, P. (1995). *Medicaid Expenditures and Beneficiaries National and State Profiles and Trends, 1984-1993.* Washington, DC: The Kaiser Commission on the Future of Medicaid.

Lou Harris and Associates (1994). *Health Care Services and Minority Groups: A*

Comparative Survey of Whites, African-Americans, Hispanics and Asian Americans. New York, NY: Lou Harris and Associates.

Moss, N., Baumeister, L., Biewener, J. (1996). Perspectives of Latina immigrant women on proposition 187. *Journal of the American Medical Women's Association 51*:161-5.

National Association of Hispanic Publications (NAHP). (1996). *Hispanic-Latinos: Diverse People in a Multicultural Society*. Washington, DC: National Association of Hispanic Publications.

National Center for Health Statistics (NCHS). (1995). *Health, United States, 1994*. Hyattsville, MD: U.S. Department of Health and Human Services, Public Health Service.

Perloff, J.D., Kletke, P., Fossett, J.W. (1995). Which physicians limit their Medicaid participation and why. *Health Services Research, 30*: 7-26.

Raffell, M.W. (1984). *Comparative Health Systems*. University Park, PA: Pennsylvania State University Press.

Rifkin, J. (1995). *The End of Work: The Decline of the Global Labor Force and the Dawn of the Post Market Era*. New York, NY: G.P. Putnam's Sons.

Shah, B.V., Barnwell, B.G., Hunt, P.N., LaVange, L.M. (1992). *SUDAAN Users Manual: Professional Software for Survey Data Analysis for Multi-Stage Designs*. Research Triangle Park, NC: Research Triangle Institute.

Schur, C.L., Bernstein, A.B., Berk, M.L. (1987). The importance of distinguishing Hispanic subpopulation in the use of medical care. *Medical Care, 25*: 627-641.

Schur, C.L., Albers, L.A., Berk, M.L. (1995). Health care use by Hispanic adults: Financial vs. non financial determinants. *Health Care Financing Review, 17*: 71-88.

Short, P.F., Cornelius, L.J., Goldstone. D.E. (1990). Health Insurance of Minorities in the United States. *Health Care for the Poor and Underserved, 1*: 9-24.

Short, P., Monheit, A., Beauregard, K. (1989). *A Profile for Uninsured Americans*. Rockville, MD: U.S. Department of Health and Human Services, Agency for Health Care Policy and Research.

Starr, P. (1982). *The Social Transformation of American Medicine*. New York: Basic Books.

U.S. Congress, Committee on Ways and Means, U.S. House of Representatives. (1994). Background material and data on major programs within the jurisdiction of the Committee on Ways and Means. Washington, DC: United States Government Printing Office.

U.S. Department of Commerce, Bureau of the Census (1998). *Statistical Abstract of the United States, 1997*. Washington, DC: United States Government Printing Office.

Vistnes J.P., Monheit A.C. (1997). *Health Insurance Status of the Civilian Noninstitutionalized Population: 1996*. Rockville, MD Agency for Health Care Policy and Research. Available: http://www.meps.ahcpr.gov/highlit/97-0030.htm.

The Structuring of Extracurricular Opportunities and Latino Student Retention

Nilda Flores-González

SUMMARY. This study examines extracurricular participation of Latino students in an inner-city high school. Multiple, intensive interviews with 33 participants, along with ethnographic observation, school records, students' transcripts, school reports, yearbooks, and other school documents were used in the research. My findings suggest that there is a strong connection between high school retention and extracurricular participation. The students who stayed in school and graduated had extracurricular participation rates much higher than students who ended up dropping out. I found that this was not due to lack of interest from non-participants but to the way extracurricular opportunities were structured. The school's formal and informal requirements for participation such as limited funds, school size, participation criteria, and access to extracurricular activities made joining the programs difficult for many students, especially those at-risk of dropping out. *[Article copies available for a fee from The Haworth Document Delivery Service: 1-800-342-9678. E-mail address: <getinfo@ haworthpressinc.com> Website: <http://www.haworthpressinc.com>]*

KEYWORDS. Extracurricular activities, high school, school retention, Latinos

While its effect is debatable, researchers agree that extracurricular participation has positive impacts on educational achievement (Finn,

---

Nilda Flores-González is affiliated with the University of Illinois at Chicago.

[Haworth co-indexing entry note]: "The Structuring of Extracurricular Opportunities and Latino Student Retention." Flores-González, Nilda. Co-published simultaneously in *Journal of Poverty* (The Haworth Press, Inc.) Vol. 4, No. 1/2, 2000, pp. 85-108; and: *Latino Poverty in the New Century: Inequalities, Challenges and Barriers* (ed: Maria Vidal de Haymes, Keith M. Kilty, and Elizabeth A. Segal) The Haworth Press, Inc., 2000, pp. 85-108. Single or multiple copies of this article are available for a fee from The Haworth Document Delivery Service [1-800-342-9678, 9:00 a.m. - 5:00 p.m. (EST). E-mail address: getinfo@haworthpressinc.com].

1989; Garbarino, 1980; Gerber, 1996; Hanks and Eckland, 1976; Goldberg and Chandler, 1989; Holland and Andre, 1987; Mahoney and Cairs, 1997; McNeal, 1995; Melnick, Sabo and Vanfossen, 1992; Murtaugh, 1988; Phillips and Schafer, 1971; Silliker and Quirk, 1997; Snyder and Spreitzer, 1992; Tinto, 1975). These studies have found that extracurricular participation decreases student alienation, raises self-esteem, increases academic performance, fosters pro-social behavior, and contributes to school retention. Given these benefits, students, especially those who are at risk of dropping out, should be encouraged, and offered the opportunity to participate in extracurricular activities. However, most students are prevented from participating due to formal and informal structural constraints placed by the school.

It is commonly believed that student interest is the driving force behind extracurricular participation. Students who are interested in extracurricular activities join these programs. Yet, far from being an open system where students match themselves to extracurricular programs according to interests and skills, these tend to be closed programs which limit participation to a selected group of students through several mechanisms. Thus, participation is not an option for many students, if not the majority of students. Many factors limit opportunities for participation in the extracurricular programs. As Quiroz, Flores-González and Frank (1996) argue, these opportunities are often structured and determined by the school itself and the sorting of students into different tracks and programs. Structural factors such as available slots, grade or skill requirements, access to information, and recruitment strategies deny the majority of students a chance to even be considered for participation.

In this article, I argue that the structuring of extracurricular activities affects retention of Latino students. Here I discuss the dynamics of extracurricular programs at a predominantly Latino inner-city high school. More precisely, I describe the benefits of extracurricular participation for the students and I explain how extracurricular activities are structured to exclude most students, and in particular those at risk of dropping out of school, from participation.

METHOD

During the 1992-93 school year, I carried out an ethnographic study at a large inner-city school in Chicago, which I named Hernández

High School. Hernández fits the image of the inner-city high school serving a low-income minority population and having a high dropout rate. At the time, the school had close to 2600 students, 83 percent of which were Latino (Chicago Public Schools, 1992). Additionally, 12.5 percent were black, 2.6 percent were Asian, and 1.8 percent were white (Chicago Public Schools, 1992). Seventy percent of the students were low-income (Chicago Public Schools, 1992). Hernández' School Report Card (Chicago Public Schools, 1992) defined low-income students as those "from families receiving public aid, living in institutions for neglected or delinquent children, being supported in foster homes with public funds or eligible to receive free or reduced-priced lunches." In addition, 21.8 percent of the students had limited English proficiency, the student mobility rate (promotion to the next grade level) was 32.5 percent, and the graduation rate was 37.1 percent (Chicago Public Schools, 1992). My calculations of the graduation and dropout rate for the class of 1993 show that 39 percent graduated, 47 percent had dropped out, and 14 percent were still in school in June 1993. In my figures, I eliminated students who left the Chicago Public School System (CPS) by transferring to private schools or public schools outside of CPS, since it was impossible to track them down. I am certain that those classified as dropouts had not re-entered school by 1993 because a request for transcripts would have been noticed in CPS files. The rates also do not reflect how many of those still in school had dropped out of school previously and re-entered into the CPS.

The purpose of my study was to find out why and how Latino students with similar backgrounds followed different educational trajectories. The study consisted of ethnographic observation at an inner-city high school and intensive interviews with 33 youths. The small sample size allowed me to gather detailed and very rich data on each participant. Of the 33 participants, 23 were students, and 10 were dropouts. I divided the students into three categories according to their educational status: stayers, leavers and returners. A stayer was someone who enrolled at Hernández as a freshman, never dropped out of school, and was a senior in 1992-93. A leaver was someone who enrolled as a freshman but left and had not re-enrolled in school as of 1992-93. A returner was someone who enrolled as a freshman at Hernández, dropped out at some point, but re-entered the school by 1992-93.

Participants were selected by two sampling methods. The stayers were selected randomly from the senior student files making sure they fit the criteria (enrolled as freshman and had never dropped out) and were willing to participate. The returners and leavers were selected through snowball sampling. I asked participants and school staff (mostly social workers and assistant principals) to provide me with names of students who had dropped out or returned to school. They often contacted potential participants and introduced me to them. The names of the participants have been changed to ensure their anonymity.

I gathered data through ethnographic observation at the school during the 1992-93 academic year. I also conducted multiple, unstructured in-depth interviews with each participant, ranging from two to ten interviews per participant. The average number of interviews with each participant was three to four. The interviews were retrospective as participants were asked about their school experiences, and other aspects of their lives, since elementary school. The interviews were tape recorded with the consent of the participants, except for five participants who requested not to be recorded. To supplement the ethnographic observation and the interviews, I also reviewed school records, students' transcripts, school reports, yearbooks, the 1993 Students' and Parents' Handbook, newsletters and other school documents.

THE SIGNIFICANCE
OF EXTRACURRICULAR PARTICIPATION

The extracurricular activities, they help keep some of the kids in school. (Jessica, a stayer)

There is no question that extracurricular participation engenders many benefits for students, and at Hernández High School this was no exception. During my field work, I found that extracurricular participation played a crucial role in shaping the experiences and educational achievement of students at Hernández. My findings suggest that extracurricular participation and student retention are inextricably linked. The students who were involved in extracurricular programs had lower dropout rates than those who did not participate. I found sharp discrepancies in the rates of extracurricular participation among the three categories of students (stayers, leavers and returners). The stayers disproportionately participated in extracurricular activities throughout their high school years while the leavers and the returners seldom did. In my sample of 33 individuals, extracurricular participation among the stayers was 85 percent in comparison to 20 percent among the leavers and 40 percent among the returners.

These findings support previous studies which assert that students who participate in extracurricular activities are less likely to drop out of school (Mahoney and Cairns, 1997; McNeal, 1995; Tinto, 1975). Mahoney and Cairns (1997) found that the dropout rate was lower among at-risk students who had participated in extracurricular activities. McNeal's (1995) research adds that although not all extracurricular activities affect student retention to the same extent, participation in athletics and fine arts programs seems to reduce the likelihood of dropping out. My findings suggest that it was not participation per se that had a positive effect on student retention at Hernández, but the many benefits students accrued as a result of participating were more important. These students had become attached to school, had developed close relationships with adults, were academic and non-academic achievers, were popular, and enjoyed school.

Some studies show that participation in extracurricular programs causes students to take on school norms and expectations, and that students who are involved in these activities exhibit pro-social behavior, value school goals, and comply with school norms (Finn, 1989; Hanks and Eckland, 1976). Although some studies find no relationship between participation and grades (Hanks and Eckland, 1976; Melnick, Sabo and Vanfossen, 1992), more recent studies suggest that extracurricular participation also has a positive effect on school performance (Gerber, 1996; Phillips and Schafer, 1971; Silliken and Quirk, 1997). At Hernández, I found that students who participated in extracurricular activities seemed to comply more readily with school norms. They had lower absentee and tardiness rates and a lower incidence of trouble with peers and staff than those who did not participate. They also maintained good academic standing, their cumulative grade point average ranging from 3.77 to 2.62, and all ranking within the top 35 percent of their graduating class (Flores-González, 1995; Flores-González, 1999).

Perhaps adherence to school norms, goals and expectations is a consequence of the attachment to school that results from participating in extracurricular programs. Students who participate in these activities come to identify with school, and its norms and expectations, because they see themselves as part of the school environment and school as part of themselves (Finn, 1989). Furthermore, participation fosters the development of other school-related identities (e.g., athlete) besides the student identity (Snyder and Spreitzer, 1992). This is consistent with what I found at Hernández, where participants in extracurricular activities exhibited other school-related identities that had become an integral part of their student identity. Eventually, the student identity was not only about attending school but also about participating in school activities. For these students, extracurricular participation became an essential part of being a student to the extent that it was difficult for them to separate their role as a student from that of a participant. For them, it was impossible to draw a line between these two identities as one was dependent on the other. For example, Ana, an athlete and stayer, was worried about possible cuts in athletic programs funding because she could not picture herself being in school and not playing sports.

> If we don't have sports, I don't know what I'll do. I like sports. I come to school to learn and play sports. If there are no sports what am I gonna do. Oh, no. I am used to playing sports, if I don't play I feel bored.

I also found that at Hernández, extracurricular programs functioned as "mini-societies" within the larger school, helping students build a sense of community. They constituted a "society" that became a group of reference. Students gained a social network consisting of peers and often sponsors, teachers or staff who supervised these groups. They fostered the growth of school-based friendships among students, making school not only a place of learning but also a place to meet with friends.

> They're [extracurricular activities] like really helpful in the way that you meet people and you get memories. . . . We're like together. . . . You're with the same people. Some people say that [school] is boring but not me because I like to learn more about people. . . . Knowing people is really good. I used to have friends but not as many as after being in scholars. (Marta, a stayer)

In addition, extracurricular activities provided Hernández' students with individualized and or small-group attention from adults. Club or program sponsors and coaches developed close and nurturing relationships with the students. They often encouraged students to take school seriously, and offered unsolicited, but often constructive, advice to students. Because they had gained the students' trust, sponsors could demand good school performance from the students. Ana, a stayer who had developed a very close relationship with her softball coach, said,

> she is not interested in sports that much. She wants you to get an education. I love that teacher so much, it's pitiful. She is not interested in sports, she coaches but she doesn't push it "you've got to play for me." If she has to choose between sports and study, she chooses study. Because you can be the best player but if you are failing a class she makes you quit and take that class. That's what I like about her. She is not like other coaches in the school that say "Well, you have to play for me." No, she is not like that. She knows that you have a future and she thinks you have to do your work and she makes you go. And that's what I like about her.

Dreeben (1968) adds that extracurricular activities provide a break from the evaluative character of classroom work because they take place outside of the classroom. They also provide an alternative route to achievement for students who are not high achievers (Finn, 1989; Murtaugh, 1988). By having the opportunity to excel outside the classroom, these students develop a sense of accomplishment and self-esteem (Garbarino, 1980; Murtaugh, 1988). According to Kinney (1993), students who participate in extracurricular activities develop a more positive personal identity. At Hernández, involvement in these programs often brought recognition and reward to the students. This was particularly crucial for students who were not academically inclined. According to Lydia, when participating "you also are recognized. Like you get a pat in the back and it makes you look forward to more things." Getting a "pat in the back" was particularly meaningful for students who did not do well academically and had low self-esteem.

Participation in extracurricular programs also provided social recognition and prestige to students in the social stratification system of the school (Hanks and Eckland, 1976; Murtaugh, 1988; Snyder and Spreitzer, 1992). It increases the participants' standing and popularity among peers. Well-known students are usually those involved in extracurricular activities, especially the athletes (Goldberg and Chandler, 1989). Because participants are recognized by others, they enjoy socio-psychological benefits that enhance their self-concept (Ornstein, 1990). Hernández was no exception to the rule as those students who participated in extracurricular activities were also the most popular in school.

> Everyone is like known. Like all the scholars are known. Like I'm in scholars, they know I'm in scholars. Like my girlfriend she is in all the athletics. They know who she is because she is in the athletics. They know the football players because they're in football. It's the season. If it's the season for football, football is more popular. If it's the season for basketball, basketball. The most popular people are the people who are in activities, extracurricular activities. Because if you are in extracurricular activities you have a bigger chance of people knowing you. (Vanessa, a stayer)

According to the students I interviewed, participation in the extracurricular diminished the monotony of school life and made school more interesting and fun. Those who participated in extracurricular activities agreed that these activities made life at school more fun, more bearable, and that their experience in school "would have been much different" if they had not participated. Alma, a stayer who participated in many extracurricular activities and was also a member of the R.O.T.C., said, "If you join clubs and join R.O.T.C., or whatever, you'll have fun. School is not boring if you make it." Even those who had dropped out of school temporarily, experienced school differently after returning because they joined extracurricular programs. Antonio, a returner, said, "I really left 'cause like the school, it was boring. I wasn't in no sports. There was nothing going on." After returning to school and joining various athletics programs, Antonio's school experience changed significantly.

> I used to be on the tumbling team, the acrobats. They stopped. . . . Then the swim team wanted me here but I left them. I don't like swimming for the school. They're slow. I can beat them, and I'm

not in the swimming team! I'll race the swimmer, one of the swimmers, and I'll beat him. 'Cause I used to swim for the park when I was a boy. I've got a lot of medals for swimming and tumbling.

By contrast, students who did not participate in extracurricular activities expressed to me feelings of alienation from school (see also Holland and Andre, 1987). Those who did not participate in extracurricular activities also said that they did not like school and felt disconnected from schools and peers. Many who eventually dropped out felt that they did not belong in school. Being temporarily out of school or absent too frequently aggravated these feelings of alienation.

And it's already hard enough for me to fit in here, not just to fit in, it's just sometimes I feel like I don't belong or something like that. It's just that lately I haven't been talking to a lot of friends. It's not that I miss them or anything but it's just there are a lot of people that like to talk to me but sometimes I don't want to talk to them. And sometimes they don't wanna talk to me. And since I've been away from school for so long, I feel like I don't belong. (Elsa, a returner)

CONSTRAINTS ON EXTRACURRICULAR PARTICIPATION

With all the benefits of extracurricular participation, it would make sense for schools to encourage widespread participation, especially among students who have marginal attachment to school. Extracurricular participation can transform the schooling experience by making school much more than a place for academic learning. Its benefits spread to the classroom, helping students develop academic, physical, and social skills. Unfortunately, schools have structured extracurricular participation in a way that not only discourages, but effectively denies most students the opportunity to participate. The four main factors that constrain widespread student participation at Hernández were limited funds, school size, participation criteria, and limited access to extracurricular activities.

Limited Funds

School funding varies greatly between urban, suburban and rural areas, and as a result students' experiences are unequal (Kozol, 1991).

This inequality is largely based on the low allocation of governmental funding per pupil and the use of local taxes to supplement the funding of schools. The more affluent a community is, the more resources it has to invest in the schools. Disparities in school funding are reflected not only in the condition of the school facilities, curriculum, and library and computer resources, but also in extracurricular opportunities. Better funded schools can afford to offer a wider range of activities while ill-funded schools have to select or restrict extracurricular offerings because of money shortages. Schools with higher expenditures per pupil have the monies needed to pay coaches and sponsors, pay membership dues to regional organizations, pay for transportation of students to and from events, and buy uniforms and equipment. By contrast, schools in poorer districts often do not have the surplus to adequately fund their existing programs. To expand beyond the basic extracurricular programs is out of the question for these schools. While schools in affluent neighborhoods offer unusual extracurricular programs along with the "basic" programs such as football and basketball, many inner-city schools have difficulties obtaining enough money to support their "basic" programs.

Inequities in school funding are only exacerbated by state cuts in school funding. These cuts have left many schools with tough decisions regarding the allocation of monies to the various school programs. Extracurricular activities are often the first programs to be affected by budget cuts. For example, during my fieldwork, CPS principals were contemplating the elimination of athletic programs for the rest of the academic year because of cuts in funding. Ultimately, they were able to salvage the athletic programs. Saving extracurricular activities in the face of budget cuts calls for creativity and initiative from schools, parents, and students who must find alternative ways to fund their programs. For instance, school districts in Montana found alternative ways, such as charging participation fees and doing fund raisers, to finance their extracurricular programs when the state legislature reduced public school funding (Morton, 1995). While charging participation fees and fund raising are viable ways to secure monies for extracurricular programs, this only exacerbates the inequity in funding. Schools in affluent areas will invariably secure more revenue for their efforts than schools in poverty stricken communities. In the former, parents can usually pay participation fees, community members have more disposable income to contribute to fund raisers, and parental and community networks often find business sponsors who can make hefty contributions to the local school. By contrast, parents and community members in low income communities simply do not possess the disposable income and business networks to procure supplemental funding for school programs.

Hernández High School is typical of the underfunded schools. It had many extracurricular programs but they were not funded adequately. Many sponsors of clubs volunteered their time and were not paid to coordinate the activities, and students had to raise money to fund their activities. Fund raisers were limited to selling small items such as candy and taffy-apples in the school's hallways. Although all extracurricular programs at Hernández were generally underfunded, this is more noticeable in the athletic programs. One major problem was the dismal state of the school's football/baseball field. The ground was so uneven that "home" games could not be played at the school's field, and students could not use the field to practice for risk of injury. In addition, funding was so scarce that athletes often had to drive themselves, take a ride, or rely on public transportation to make it to their meets because the school did not have money to pay for a bus. A side effect of the lack of funding was that the general student population did not have the opportunity to participate as spectators of their school team, even in "home" games.

School Size

In large high schools, those with student populations of over 700, students have fewer opportunities to participate in extracurricular activities. Coladarci and Cobb (1996) report higher rates of extracurricular participation among students in schools with less than 800 students, and lower rates of participation in school with more than 1600 students. The larger the school, the more negative its effects on student satisfaction, attendance, identification with school, and behavior (Fowler and Walberg, 1991; Ornstein, 1990). According to Ornstein (1990):

> a school is considered too large when a loss of personal or school identity among students occurs; they are unable to fully participate in social and athletic activities or have difficulty interacting among themselves or feel they do not belong to the student body or school in general. (p. 239)

A lower proportion of students participate in extracurricular activities in large schools in comparison to small schools. Although large schools have more extracurricular programs than smaller schools, they also have more people competing for slots in these programs (Barker and Gump, 1964; Morgan and Alwin, 1980). Having many students to choose from in the large schools, average students, students that are not talented, are easily overlooked (Ornstein, 1990). Because there are fewer students in the smaller schools, even marginal students are needed and encouraged to fill the slots in the extracurricular activities (Barker and Gump, 1964; Garbarino and Brofenbrenner, 1976). As a result, students in smaller schools participate more often and in a greater variety of extracurricular activities than students in large schools (Barker and Gump, 1964; Pittman and Haughwout, 1987).

While participating in extracurricular programs fosters connections to school, only a limited number of students engaged in these activities at Hernández. An examination of extracurricular participation at Hernández for four academic years yielded similar results (see Flores-González, 1995; Quiroz, 1993; Quiroz, Flores-González and Frank, 1996). These studies found that there were slots in the extracurricular programs for 25 percent of the student population. That is, 650 slots were open for a student population of 2600. However, in 1992-93, only 19 percent of students, or 494 students, actually participated in these programs. This disparity is due to students' participation in more than one extracurricular activity. As a result, 2106 students did not participate in extracurricular activities!

I found that at Hernández the participation rate varied by grade level. Among those who participated, 19 percent were freshmen, 25 percent sophomores, 29 percent juniors, and 27 percent seniors. This gives the impression that participation is spread out rather equally throughout the grade levels. Yet because each cohort has a different size, due to high dropout and grade repetition rates, participation is not equally distributed throughout the grade levels. In fact, there were 714 freshmen, 727 sophomores, 852 juniors and 298 seniors during 1992-93. Looking at the rate of participation in each grade level, a disproportionate number of the seniors were participating compared to other cohorts: 13 percent of the freshmen, 17 percent of the sophomores, 17 percent of the juniors, and 44 percent of the seniors. This is more striking when taking into consideration that the senior class is only 11.5 percent of the student population. The pattern of increasing rates of extracurricular participation throughout the years suggests that there may be a connection between participating and staying in school. Especially, the finding that such a disproportionate number of the seniors participate suggests that those who participate are the ones who stay in school and graduate. In fact, most of the stayers told me that they had been involved in extracurricular programs prior to their senior year. Thus, the high participation rate among seniors appears to have more to do with the higher retention of students who participate in extracurricular programs than to an increase in participation during the senior year.

As I indicated earlier, I found that extracurricular participation varied among the three status groupings, with the stayers having the highest rate of participation (85 percent) while the returners and the leavers had low rates (40 percent and 20 percent, respectively). These rates reflect participation since their freshman year, showing that the stayers have consistently participated at a higher rate than the other groups. There were also other differences among these groups. The stayers' participation included the complete range of activities at the school (e.g., intellectual, athletics, academic clubs, social clubs, professional clubs), while the leavers' and returners' participation was limited to athletics and academic clubs. The only returner who participated in athletics had been cut from the team because of poor grades whereas the leavers and returners who participated in academic clubs did so only because they were enrolled in a class with an extracurricular component, such as band. Another difference between these status groups rests in the number of activities they participated in. The stayers participated in at least one of these activities and most of them participated in three or more activities for more than one school year. In one case, a stayer participated in 13 extracurricular activities in her senior year! By contrast, the leavers and returners often participated in none. While it seems that the stayers monopolized most openings in the extracurricular programs, it was the way the school structured extracurricular opportunities which limited access of other students to extracurricular programs.

Participation Criteria at Hernández

Extracurricular programs are viewed as open systems where everyone has an equal chance to participate. In reality, schools place many constraints that curtail widespread student participation. Extracurricular participation is a privilege and not a right. Students are not entitled to participate, they must earn the privilege to participate. To be eligible for participation they have to meet certain requirements. At Hernández, grades, enrollment in classes, and skill level were the "objective" criteria used to admit students in the extracurricular programs.

Grades

At Hernández, the main criterion for participation was grades. Although some studies find no relationship between extracurricular participation and grades (Hanks and Eckland, 1976; Melnick, Sabo and Vanfossen, 1992), grades are used as a prerequisite for participation. Grade requirements, popularly known as the "no pass/no play" rule or the "C-average" policy, normally require students to pass all their classes or maintain a grade point average of 2.0 (Bland, 1990; O'Reilly, 1992).

> I wanted to be in the Pom Pons team but since I had F's, you can't be in no [extracurricular] program unless you have a C average or better. And since I had two F's I couldn't try out. That's the only thing I would be interested in. (Diana, a returner)

Not only were students who failed to obtain good grades denied entry into extracurricular programs, but they were expelled from them if their grades deteriorated below a C grade point average. Jerry, a returner, said, "I used to play basketball, actually I played for two years. I played baseball but I got cut because [of] my grades. That's about the only two sports I was playing."

Enrollment in Classes/Programs

While some students sought to participate in extracurricular activities, many students ended up in them incidentally. This happened while taking classes or enrolling in academic programs that had extracurricular components. Extracurricular activities, such as the physics club, choir, band, and R.O.T.C. were restricted to students enrolled in these particular classes. Students received credit for taking the classes and at the same time took part in extracurricular programs. Not all students enrolled in these courses because they were interested in them. Many enrolled to fulfill graduation requirements, or simply to avoid other classes. For example, many students enrolled in R.O.T.C. not because of interest but as an alternative to physical education. Most students enrolled in classes like band or choir just because they had to complete a number of credits in the various subject areas. Diana, a returner, explained, "I was in band but that's because it was my music credit. Otherwise, I wouldn't have been either." While some students came to enjoy these classes because of the extracurricular components, many complained that the diversity of students with different interests and at different skill levels made these classes slow and boring.

Other extracurricular activities required membership in specific academic programs. For example, members of the Anchor and Key clubs had to be enrolled in the advanced academic program. Some activities heavily recruited from particular academic programs, although participation was not restricted to these programs. For example, although the New Americans and the Spanish clubs were heavily populated by students from the Bilingual program, other students could also participate but often did not.

Skills

Some extracurricular programs required a minimum skill level for admission. These were more notably the sports programs, for which students had to compete with other students for the limited slots in the teams. One would assume that in a school like Hernández, with 2600 students, competition would be fierce. Yet, few students actually went to the try outs, and none of the students I interviewed said they had been rejected because of competition. Rejection was usually the result of not having the required grade point average. In other programs, such as advanced band and advanced choir, skill level was not always strictly enforced. Because students at different skill levels are bunched together in these classes, those with advanced skills eventually lost interest because the class became too elementary for them. For instance, Ana, a stayer who had played the clarinet since elementary school eventually became utterly bored with band because she was required to play simple pieces that her less skilled peers could play.

> I like playing, I just don't like the band. . . . He [teacher] gives us music for little kids, tutututu. I don't like that. I tell him to pick

this and this and this. [He says] "No, it's too hard for all of you."
We should be knowing how to play it. (Ana, a stayer)

Limiting Access to Extracurricular Programs

While the structural requirements for participation such as grades,
class/program enrollment, and skill level give the impression that the
extracurricular program was fair and that anyone who met the "objective" criteria (grades, class enrollment, and skills) was eligible, I
found that other "informal" factors made competition for extracurricular activities an unfair and unequal system in which most students did
not stand a chance. There were subtleties in the extracurricular system
of which students were unaware but which restricted access to extracurricular opportunities. These informal constraints included access to
information about extracurricular opportunities, recruitment into programs, and the peer group.

Access to Information

Access to information was a valuable yet a scarce resource at
Hernández, where many students did not find out about extracurricular
opportunities. Opportunities to join were rarely announced publicly
through the school loudspeaker, newsletters, or fliers. Consequently,
most students were not aware of application deadlines or try-outs.
Even when announcements were made over the loudspeaker system,
many students simply could not hear them because of malfunctioning
loudspeakers in their classrooms. In addition, few teachers bothered to
make announcements to their students.

Another vehicle for disseminating information about school activities was the school newsletter. However, at Hernández there were
several problems with the school newsletter. The school-wide newsletter was published sporadically, thus many events were not announced
in it. In addition, its distribution was disorganized. Nobody knew
when the next issue would be out, and not everyone received a copy of
it. To make matters worse, the newsletter often announced events that
had already happened or with too short a notice for students to be able
to make arrangements to attend. Another problem with the newsletter
was that other groups within the school had their own newsletter
which only added to the confusion of where to find and post information.

Fliers were often used to post information about athletic team try-outs or other extracurricular program deadlines. However, there was no centralized bulletin board where school announcements could be posted. Thus, fliers were posted on walls throughout the school, yet few students noticed them, and if they noticed, they did not have the time to read them. In a school with 2600 students, the halls were packed during class changes and it was impossible for a student to stand and read a flier while others students were pushing and the hall monitors were telling them to keep moving.

Recruitment

Recruitment into extracurricular programs was not made on an equal opportunity basis because at Hernández students were selectively recruited into them. Many students were recruited into extracurricular activities by teachers and the sponsors of the activities. Teachers informed particular students about opportunities and often asked them to join activities that they sponsored. For instance, Lydia, a stayer, participated in Future Business Leaders of America because the teacher asked her to join since she needed a certain number of students to obtain funding.

Students were also recruited into academic programs by teachers and counselors, especially into the Scholars Program, the advanced placement program. Many *scholars,* as participants were called, were recruited by high school counselors while they were still in eighth grade. Selection was based on their high grades and exam scores. Other *scholars* were recruited after their freshman year because of outstanding performance in their classes.

> My freshman year I was doing real good and my division [home room] teacher was like "You've got to get into honors classes. That's really good for you." I was like "No, 'cause I'm gonna mess up." So sophomore year, my other division teacher was like "You gotta get in, you gotta get in." So when I went to pick my classes for junior year my counselor was like "You wanna get in?" I'm like "Man, everybody is telling me about it but I don't want to 'cause I'm gonna mess up." And she said, "No, with your brain and your intelligence and your accurateness and everything. You're not gonna mess up if you put your head set on it." So she got me in, and that's how it started. (Marta, a stayer)

As Marta's quote conveys, sometimes teachers and counselors were adamant in recruiting students into their extracurricular programs. They continued to insist until they convinced the student to join. Of course, recruitment was very selective since the teachers and counselors encouraged only the "good" kids to join these programs. That is, students who were asked to join tended to be good students who did not cause any trouble. Students perceived to be troublemakers were simply not asked to join.

Peers

Some students joined extracurricular programs because a friend persuaded them to participate, or they simply wanted to be with their friends. For instance, Elizabeth became a *scholar* because her friends, who were *scholars,* pressured her to join, and because she persistently asked a counselor to let her in.

> . . . since sophomore year I always took honor classes and I was with them [Scholars] always. . . . [My Scholar friends would say] "Go do it" and I did. Because they were all Scholars, only like three of them were not Scholars, and I would go to the meetings. . . . So I talked to the counselor . . . and she said "Elizabeth, you have to come to my office. You have to sign these papers." And it was for that. And that's how I got in. (Elizabeth, a scholar)

As in the example above, students tended to participate in extracurricular programs where their peers concentrate. Students seldom ventured into extracurricular programs on their own.

At Hernández, the student stratification system usually dictated which extracurricular activities were permissible to each individual. This was most noticeable in the "main sports" at the school. Athletes, particularly those in the main sports like girls' volleyball, girls' softball, boys' football, and boys' baseball, tended to hang out together and were highly visible in school. They constituted an elite clique within the school which monopolized and seemed to control participation in teams. Many participated in more than one sport. For instance, Ana, a stayer, played volleyball, basketball, and softball. The cliquish nature of sports culture at Hernández and their control over the main sports programs may have deterred other students from participating more than the actual "official" requirements.

The cliquish nature of sports at Hernández was also evident in the ethnic composition of the athletic programs, especially in the boys' teams. Puerto Ricans and other Caribbeans (Dominicans and Cubans) dominated the "main sports" of football and baseball. African American students, both boys and girls, were usually found on the basketball teams, while students of Mexican and Central American origin (Guatemala, Honduras, El Salvador and Nicaragua) made up the boys' soccer team.

Because peer groups tended to form among students in the same academic tracks and programs, it was not surprising that students from the same academic track or program tended to concentrate in particular extracurricular activities. According to Quiroz, Flores-González and Frank (1996), educational tracking lets schools structure the educational experiences of students, and provides them with different opportunities including extracurricular opportunities.

DISCUSSION

This study suggests that there is a strong connection between high school retention and extracurricular participation. I found that students who stayed in school and graduated had extracurricular participation rates much higher than students who ended up dropping out. Although dropouts participated less and showed less interest in extracurricular participation, the data shows that their lower participation was more likely due to the school's structural constraints that impeded their participation than to their lack of interest. The school's formal and informal requirements for participation were difficult, and often impossible, to meet by many students.

Some factors that limit student participation, such as school funding and size of the school, are system-wide and require state and local legislation to change. What individual schools can do to offset the adverse effects of funding and school size is limited and constrained by other factors in the community such as social class. That is, schools in more affluent areas can more easily generate supplemental funds to finance programs or even expand school facilities than schools in low income areas. Affluent communities also have more political clout and connections, and thus are more effective in lobbying for their schools. Even in large school systems, such as the Chicago Public Schools, more affluent neighborhoods tend to house the "magnet" or academically specialized schools while general education and vocational high schools are usually located in low-income communities. Schools in low-income areas must often resort to mass mobilizations to demand more resources, or to seek funding through grants or partnerships with business and local universities that can provide services at no cost to the school. Although seeking out and implementing these alternatives requires much time and energy from the school administration and faculty, they can lead to the expansion of extracurricular offerings with a minimal burden on the school financial resources.

Another relatively inexpensive way to expand extracurricular programs is by getting more teachers involved in the development and sponsorship of these programs. Normally, schools pay teachers a stipend for their extracurricular programs, especially athletic coaches. Therefore, teachers can be enticed to sponsor extracurricular programs through monetary rewards. However, at schools with low financial resources this is often not an option. The only viable way to staff these programs is by enlisting teachers to participate voluntarily. Perhaps schools could offer non-monetary incentives, such as recognition and awards, for teachers who sponsor extracurricular programs.

As if getting teachers to volunteer their time was not hard enough, the increasing apathy found among teachers in inner-city schools adds to the problem. While Hernández High School had a significant number of teachers who volunteered to sponsor extracurricular activities, most teachers had no desire or sense of obligation to do this work. These teachers showed up to teach, had no interaction with students outside of the classroom and seldom attended any school functions. One of these teachers, who was close to retirement, told me that he used to sponsor a science club. He stopped doing so when the student population changed and he felt that the students did not have any interest in such programs. His vision of this generation of students led him to remove himself from any extracurricular involvement. Unfortunately, many teachers shared his view. The challenge is then to change teachers' perceptions of the students and instill in them a sense of commitment to their schools and the community.

Other factors affecting student extracurricular participation are institutional practices that can be modified to provide equitable extracurricular opportunities to all students. For instance, changes in the participation criteria can open the extracurricular programs to more students. While formal criteria such as skill level and class or program enrollment limit participation in some extracurricular areas, grade requirements do not need to be the defining requirement. Research shows that involvement in extracurricular activities increases academic performance. So, why restrict participation to those who are already doing well in school? If participation leads to increasing grades, then students who are academically weak, and especially at-risk students, should be allowed and encouraged to participate.

Although the "no pass/no play" rule restricts participation, many students who meet the formal criteria (grades, skill level) still do not participate. These students' participation is hindered by the informal constraints to extracurricular participation of which they are unaware. Lack of information, teachers' selective recruiting practices, and the peer group contribute to the unequal distribution of extracurricular opportunities. Schools can take steps to ensure that information about extracurricular participation is distributed among the student population and not funneled to a select group of students. It can also encourage, and even require, teachers not to limit their recruitment to the "good" kids but also to recruit among the at-risk students for their programs. Peer groups, especially marginal groups, can be encouraged and recruited to participate as a group.

It is particularly crucial that schools restructure the way extracurricular programs function not only to retain students but also to enhance the schooling experience of its students. I found that students who participated in these programs were generally satisfied with their school experience, and they attributed their positive attitudes towards school to their participation. Extracurricular participation attached them to a "mini-society" within the larger school community where they developed close relationships with peers and the adult sponsors. Participating also made them feel good because it often elicited recognition and rewards such as increased prestige among their peers. The positive effect of extracurricular participation was evident in their pro-social behavior such as maintaining good academic standing and following school norms. Although not presented in this article, I found that these students had low rates of absenteeism, class cutting, and antisocial behavior at school (see Flores-González, 1995). By contrast, those who did not participate found school boring and displayed many signs of their discontent. These students had little connection to school which became evident in their selection of non-school-oriented peers and problematic behavior at school. They often cut classes, were absent, obtained low grades, or were experiencing other troubles at school. These behaviors may explain their lower participation rates but these rates are compounded by the manner in which the school-structured opportunities reinforced their behavior and closed doors.

Since extracurricular participation has the potential of transforming the schooling experience of youth and contributing to the retention of students, they should be fostered by schools. We cannot expect students to become engaged in school, especially when schools offer little more than academics. The "return to the basics" movement argues that students should spend more time in the classroom and less in non-academic activities. Yet, this has been happening in most inner-city schools where extracurricular opportunities are scant to begin with. Still, reading and math scores are low, attendance is erratic, and the dropout rate is soaring. By contrast, it is in the schools that have more extracurricular offerings where test scores are high and most students not only graduate but attend college. Although extracurricular activities are not the only solution to enhancing the school experience, they are important and often overlooked factors that have the potential to engage students in learning and motivate them to stay in school.

REFERENCES

Barker, R. and Gump, V. (1964). *Big school, small school: High school size and student behavior.* Stanford, CA: Stanford University Press.

Bland, J. (1990). *Implementation of the c-average policy* (ED331932). ERIC. Chicago Public Schools. (1992). *School Report Card.*

Coladarci, T., & Cobb, C. D. (1996). Extracurricular participation, school size, and achievement and self-esteem among high school students: A national look. *Journal of Research in Rural Education, 12*(2), 92-103.

Dreeben, R. (1968). *On what is learned in school.* Reading, MA: Addison-Wesley.

Finn, J. D. (1989). Withdrawing from school. *Review of Educational Research, 59*(2), 117-142.

Flores-González, N. M. (1995). *Diverging educational paths: Sustenance, exit, and reentry into the student role.* Unpublished doctoral dissertation, University of Chicago, Chicago, IL.

Flores-González, N. (1999). Puerto Rican high achievers: An example of ethnic and academic identity compatibility. *Anthropology and Education Quarterly, 30*(3), 1-20.

Fowler, W. J., & Walberg, H. J. (1991). School size, characteristics, and outcomes. *Educational Evaluation and Policy Analysis, 13*(2), 189-202.

Garbarino, J. (1980). Some thoughts on school size and its effects on adolescent development. *Journal of Youth and Adolescence, 9*(1), 19-31.

Garbarino, J., & Bronfenbrenner, U. (1976). The socialization of moral judgement and behavior in cross-cultural perspective. In T. Lickona (Ed.), *Moral development and behavior.* New York: Holt, Rinehart and Winston.

Gerber, S. B. (1996). Extracurricular activities and academic achievement. *Journal of Research and Development in Education, 30*(1), 42-50.

Goldberg, A. D., & Chandler, T. J. L. (1989). The role of athletics: The social world of high school adolescents. *Youth & Society, 21*(2), 238-250.

Hanks, M. P., & Eckland, B. K. (1976). Athletics and social participation in the educational attainment process. *Sociology of Education, 49,* 271-294.

Holland, A., & Andre, T. (1987). Participation in extracurricular activities in secondary school: What is known, what needs to be known? *Review of Educational Research, 51*(4), 437-466.

Kinney, D. (1993). From nerds to normals: The recovery of identity among adolescents from middle school to high school. *Sociology of Education, 66,* 21-40.

Kozol, J. (1991). *Savage inequalities: Children in American schools.* NY: Crown Publishers.

Mahoney, J., & Cairs, R. B. (1997). Do extracurricular activities protect against early school dropout? *Developmental Psychology, 33,* 241-53.

McNeal, R. B. (1995). Extracurricular activities and high school dropouts. *Sociology of Education, 68,* 62-81.

Melnick, M. J., Sabo, D. F., & Vanfossen, B. (1992). Educational effects of interscholastic athletic participation on African-American and Hispanic youth. *Adolescence, 27*(106), 295-308.

Morgan, D. L., & Alwin, D. F. (1980). When less is more: School size and student social participation. *Social Psychology Quarterly, 43*(2), 241-252.

Morton, C. (1995). *Creativity versus dollars: How rural schools in one state have maintained or improved their extra-curricular programs in the face of funding cuts* (ED389499). ERIC.

Murtaugh, M. (1988). Achievement outside the classroom: The role of nonacademic activities in the lives of high school students. *Anthropology & Education Quarterly, 19,* 382-395.

O'Reilly, J. M. (1992). *Did the kids win or lose? The impact of 'no pass/no play' rule on student achievement* (ED357410). ERIC.

Ornstein, A. C. (1990). School size and effectiveness: Policy implications. *The Urban Review, 22*(3), 239-245.

Phillips, J. C., & Schafer, W. E. (1971). Consequences of participation in interscholastic sports: A review and prospects. *Pacific Sociological Review, 14*(3), 328-338.

Pittman, R. B., & Haughwout, P. (1987). Influence of high school size on dropout rate. Educational Evaluation and Policy Analysis, 9(4), 337-343.

Quiroz, P. A. (1993). *A study of decision-making in the educational process of Latino high school students.* Unpublished doctoral dissertation, University of Chicago, Chicago, IL.

Quiroz, P. A., Flores-González, N., & Frank, K. (1996). Carving a niche in the high school social structure: Formal and informal constraints on participation in the extra curriculum. In A. Pallas (Ed.), *Research in sociology of education and socialization, 11* (pp. 93-120). Greenwich: CT: JAI Press.

Silliker, S. A., & Quirk, J. T. (1997). The effect of extracurricular activity participation on the academic performance of male and female high school students. *The School Counselor, 44*, 288-293.

Snyder, E. E., & Spreitzer, E. (1992). Social psychological components of adolescents' role identities as scholars and athletes: A longitudinal analysis. *Youth & Society, 23*(4), 507-522.

Tinto, V. (1975). Dropouts from higher education: A theoretical synthesis of recent research. *Review of Educational Research, 45*, 89-125.

Politics, Networks, and Circular Migration: The Salvadoran Experience

José Soltero
Romeo Saravia

SUMMARY. This paper examines the relevance of individual and structural theories of migration for Salvadoran circular migrants to the U.S. and other countries. Using 1995 individual data taken from impoverished suburban areas corresponding to cities across the fourteen Salvadoran geographic departments, our results strongly support the importance of network theories of migration. Thus, the existence of networks of support in the U.S. increases individuals' migration likelihood; in contrast, attachment to networks in the sending country, such as community organizations, decreases people's probability to become circular migrants to any country. Finally, contrary to hypothetical expectations, political factors do not influence our sample's migration patterns. *[Article copies available for a fee from The Haworth Document Delivery Service: 1-800-342-9678. E-mail address: <getinfo@haworthpressinc.com> Website: <http://www.haworthpressinc.com>]*

José Soltero is affiliated with the Department of Sociology, DePaul University.

Romeo Saravia is affiliated with the Human Rights Institute, University of El Salvador.

Address correspondence to: José Soltero, Department of Sociology, DePaul University, 2320 N. Kenmore Avenue, Chicago, IL 60614.

The authors want to thank John Koval, Felix Masud-Piloto, Mike Mezey, Rose Spalding, Maria Vidal de Haymes, Rafaela Weffer, Sonia White, and two anonymous reviewers for their help.

This research was funded by grants from the University Research Council and the Liberal Arts and Sciences College at DePaul University, and supported by the University of El Salvador, the Department of Sociology and Academic Affairs' Faculty Development Seminar in Central America, also at DePaul University.

[Haworth co-indexing entry note]: "Politics, Networks, and Circular Migration: The Salvadoran Experience." Soltero, José, and Romeo Saravia. Co-published simultaneously in *Journal of Poverty* (The Haworth Press, Inc.) Vol. 4, No. 1/2, 2000, pp. 109-130; and: *Latino Poverty in the New Century: Inequalities, Challenges and Barriers* (ed: Maria Vidal de Haymes, Keith M. Kilty, and Elizabeth A. Segal) The Haworth Press, Inc., 2000, pp. 109-130. Single or multiple copies of this article are available for a fee from The Haworth Document Delivery Service [1-800-342-9678, 9:00 a.m. - 5:00 p.m. (EST). E-mail address: getinfo@haworthpressinc.com].

KEYWORDS. Networks, Salvadoran, migration

INTRODUCTION

Three types of immigrants are currently considered in immigration studies: economic migrants, political migrants, and refugees. The first group is looking to improve their economic well-being in countries that offer a higher salary, more jobs, and a higher standard of living. The second group, although they may share some of the reasons of the former economic migrants, is also leaving their country of origin because of their disappointment with governmental policy outcomes. Finally, the third group, the refugees, has to abandon their country because they fear for their life.

However, it is difficult to distinguish between economic or political motivations among the immigrants to the U.S. due to the lack of appropriate data to test between economic and political reasons for migration (de la Garza & Szekely, 1997, pp. 218-219). The relevance of political reasons to emigrate have been argued by several authors as some of the most important motivations to exit a country (Hamilton & Stoltz-Chinchilla, 1997, pp. 81-96). Thus, Salvadoran migration to the U.S. has been considered as having a very significant political component due to the civil war in which El Salvador was immersed during the 1970s, 1980s, and the early 1990s (Sassen, 1995a, pp. 274-275).

In this study, we analyze the relative importance of political and economic migration among Salvadoran circular or return migrants to the U.S. and other countries–defined as those Salvadoran individuals who have spent any amount of time in a foreign country and have returned to El Salvador. To this end, our study uses data gathered in fourteen impoverished suburban areas or shantytowns of El Salvador during 1995. These zones suffered "[t]he combined effects of political crisis, war, and the economic crisis aggravated by political conditions [which] have transformed a normal migration flow into massive displacement and exodus. In terms of internal displacement, it has been estimated that by 1987 up to a million Central Americans (including a quarter-million Nicaraguans, one hundred thousand to a quarter-million Guatemalans, and half a million Salvadorans) had been displaced within their own countries" (Hamilton & Stoltz-Chinchilla, 1997, p. 90). According to Americas Watch (1991, p. 108), a significant amount of these displaced individuals have entered the United States as illegal aliens. It has been estimated that the number of immigrants from El Salvador is more than a half million since 1980.

Nevertheless, Mexican immigration has been the most studied case of migration (Bean, de la Garza, Roberts, & Weintraub, 1997) because Mexicans are the largest group of immigrants to the U.S. (Gelbard & Carter, 1997, p. 134). However, the study of Salvadoran immigration to the U.S. is also of central importance, not only theoretically, but also empirically. Indeed, the U.S. receives 52% of emigration from El Salvador (Sassen, 1995a, p. 275), a country that also sends to the U.S. the second largest–only after México–contingent of undocumented immigrants (Portes & Rumbaut, 1996, p. 275). Furthermore, people of Central and South American origin represent the fastest growing and most diverse segment of the Latino community in the U.S. (Schaefer & Lamm, 1997, p. 196). Sociologists Hamilton and Stoltz-Chinchilla (1997, p. 91) assert that "the number of undocumented Salvadorans apprehended doubled between 1977 and 1981 from eight to sixteen thousand and reached seventeen thousand in 1985 (data from the INS)." In addition, Ruggles and Fix (1985, pp. 45-47) estimate that three-quarters of a million to 1.3 million Central American migrants are living in the United States, two-thirds of them Salvadorans, and up to one-fifth Guatemalans. Finally, the U.S. General Accounting Office (GAO) estimates the number of undocumented Salvadorans in the United States at six to eight hundred thousand (U.S. General Accounting Office, 1989).

Therefore, if indeed economic and political factors are relevant to explain Salvadoran circular migration to the U.S. and other countries, it is still necessary to investigate precisely what economic and political social traits or individual characteristics are significant determinants of migration likelihood. Hence, in the first section that follows we present a brief review of migration theories in order to obtain a group of hypotheses relevant to circular migration from El Salvador. Next, we introduce the data and methods used to test the former hypotheses. The third section discusses the findings in relation to the hypotheses laid out above. Finally, the last section summarizes and concludes the analysis.

DETERMINANTS OF MIGRATION

Two main perspectives predominate among migration theories. The first focuses on push-pull factors that essentially affect individuals, and the second prioritizes structural social constructs that influence groups of individuals. The first model of push-pull forces of immigration has a remarkable affinity with the cost-benefit approach to immigration explained by some labor economists; it supports the idea that greater disadvantages–factors of expulsion–will naturally lead to greater migration as individuals try to escape their situation (Borjas, 1990; Thomas, 1973). These factors of expulsion may include unemployment, underemployment, poverty, and landlessness.

The structural perspective on migration includes macrostructural and microstructural dimensions. The former focuses on the structural imbalances that core societies impose over peripheral and semi-peripheral ones by means of colonial or neocolonial relations of trade and production (Portes & Rumbaut, 1997, pp. 272-276). The structural imbalances include the change of production and trade patterns, such as the extension of private property and capitalist ways of land exploitation in rural areas, which in turn result in the displacement of peasants toward cities and other countries. Such structural imbalances may lead to political cleavages, including civil wars, that produce dense flows of migration in a short term (Masud-Piloto, 1996; Portes & Rumbaut, 1996, p. 275; Sassen, 1995b, p. 282).

Political migration, thus, is seen by this perspective as the result of the failure of the political system to incorporate and respond to publicly articulated demands for participation and policy in ways that reflect governmental accountability and responsiveness. Individuals whose suggestions or preferences are never taken into account or continuously rejected may become alienated, and in consequence could mobilize or threaten the state via urban protests or guerrilla movements, but may also choose to emigrate (Hirschman, 1970).

Refugees, then, are distinct from political and economic migrants. "Refugees either flee widespread but untargeted violence such as occurs during any revolution, or they emigrate to escape persecution" (de la Garza & Szekely, 1997, p. 204). Economic migrants leave attracted by the idea of improving their economic conditions and are unconcerned about political processes. In El Salvador, since 1979, "at least one fourth of the entire population of the country has had to abandon possessions, homes, and communities; many have had to endure separation from family members and friends. These separations have often become permanent" (Americas Watch, 1991, p. 107). In addition, this structural perspective also analyzes the role of influential groups in the receiving country; employers, unions, as well as the legislation reforms enforced by the states in order to control migration flows (Granovetter, 1995, pp. 128-157; Portes, 1995, pp. 248-275; Roberts & Escobar, 1997, pp. 47-71; Sassen, 1995a, pp. 87-118; Weintraub, 1997, pp. 284-296).

The microstructural dimension of this perspective centers on the relevance of social networks for migration. "Once an external event such as the presence of labor recruiters or the diffusion of information about economic opportunities abroad triggers the departure of a few pioneering migrants, the migration process may become self-sustaining through the construction of increasingly dense social ties across space" (Portes & Rumbaut, 1997, p. 276). Thus, for this perspective the role of circular migrants is of paramount importance since they disseminate the information that may facilitate the journey of others.

Therefore, having limited our study to the impoverished suburban population of El Salvador (see the next section), the following hypotheses, inferred from the migration theories discussed above, can be tested:

Hypothesis 1. The likelihood of migration for individuals–circular or otherwise–is increased by unemployment, underemployment, landlessness, poverty, and other forms of personal *economic* hardship.

Hypothesis 2. The availability of support networks at the receiving country increases the migration likelihood of individuals. Alternatively, attachment to social groups within the sending countries decreases the likelihood of migration.

Hypothesis 3. Political supporters of radical, alternative, or anti-government political groups are more likely than non-supporters to engage in migration.

Hypothesis 4. Individuals living in those regions within a country that are more affected by political unrest or violence are more likely to migrate than others living in less conflictive areas.

In the following section, we introduce the data and methods necessary to test the former hypotheses.

DATA AND METHODS

Focusing on fourteen Salvadoran municipalities (Appendix), a random sample of households was taken from each municipality's impoverished suburban area by surveying a randomly chosen portion of the peripheral zone of each town, areas which in part are constituted by shanty towns formed by adobe or cardboard shacks, during April to September 1995. We were assisted by a team of interviewers composed of ten senior-year law students working on this project to satisfy their social service requirement for graduation at the University of El Salvador. During the period of the survey, none of these students were members of the FMLN, ARENA, or any other political party or organization. In addition, our previous talks and discussions with these potential interviewers indicated that they were not interested in supporting or advancing any political agenda or ideology.

In our survey, members of households who were sixteen years old or older were interviewed, including persons of the extended family. Thus, using a written questionnaire, individual information was collected for a sample of 1,487 cases. In a few cases, the family inhabiting a house was not present or there was only a minor at the house when the interview was requested. In these cases, as well as during interview rejections, another household was randomly selected in the area as a substitute for the missing one. In addition, the interviewers were provided with identification cards and official letters from the University of El Salvador to show to the potential interviewees when asking for the interview. Only less than 3% of the total individuals asked for an interview opted for a rejection and in all these cases the reason was lack of time. An additional 2% of the households did not have an adult present at the moment of the interview and had to be substituted.

The survey contains information on age, gender, migration, employment, education, land ownership, housing conditions, health, health services, political participation, and voting behavior. Since the questionnaire asks individuals about their political support and membership in the FMLN, our team was concerned that people would fear political or physical repression by admitting their collaboration with the FMLN. For example, political assassinations were still happening–several ex-commandants of the FMLN were murdered between 1993 and 1994: Oscar Grimaldi, Hernan Castro, Carlos Velez, and Mario Lopez; attempts against Nidia Diaz were also made on two occasions–these attacks were very selective against the current or former leaders of the FMLN (Cordova-Macias, 1996, p. 34). Overall, Salvadorans FMLN activists were out in the open, as Montgomery (1995) attests:

The cease fire, which began unofficially on December 31 [1992], became formal on February 1 and was heralded with a national celebration. FMLN supporters were everywhere, sporting red bandanas. About 1,000 showed up at the airport on January 31 to welcome FMLN leaders who flew in on a Mexican air force plane and from Managua on a U.N. aircraft. A ceremony was held on February 1 to install the National Commission for the Consolidation of Peace (COPAZ); FMLN members who had not been seen in public in twelve years were in the audience; clandestine supporters were seen openly fraternizing with FMLN members to the surprise, even shock, of many. In the afternoon and evening the FMLN celebrated in the Plaza Civica, in front of the cathedral where the 1979 massacre and the violence at Archbishop Romero's funeral had occurred. The cathedral was draped with an enormous banner that bore the image of Monseigneur Romero and the words "You are resurrected in your people." Radio Venceremos broadcast live from the plaza. (p. 225)

Nevertheless, a pilot study to check for potential response problems was conducted in the municipalities of Ahuachapan and San Salvador, two municipalities where the FMLN allegedly does not have a strong political support relative to other political parties, such as the Nationalist Republican Alliance (ARENA) (Moreno-Parada, 1994, pp. 110-111). Given that the results of the pilot survey did not indicate interviewees abnormal reticence to be interviewed nor to answer about their political views or political participation, the team decided to proceed with the survey in the remaining Salvadoran departments, the equivalent of U.S. states. As it turned out, the individuals interviewed were quite forthright in answering the questions regarding their political preferences and participation. None of the individuals interviewed hesitated to answer about their membership in the FMLN, but 3% did not express any conviction about supporting any political party. In addition, all individuals answered the question on union membership, but 1.1% did not want to answer the question related to land ownership; similarly, 2.4% did not want to express their religious affiliation or employment status, 5.9% did not know if they had any relatives in the U.S. or did not want to answer, and 17% did not want to answer if they had been in the U.S. or did not know they had stepped temporarily into a neighboring country, such as Honduras, while escaping the ravages of the civil war. Thus, more individuals were likely to answer about political participation than having kinship in the U.S. or migration. In part this is due to several individuals' lack of knowledge regarding their relatives' death, migration, or disappearance during the civil war. It is also plausible that some individuals may believe that by answering this question they may hurt their migration prospects.

Defining a circular or return migrant as an individual sixteen years old or older who has been in the U.S. or in any other country for any period of time and has returned to El Salvador, even if such an individual had been detained and deported upon arrival by the INS, two logistic regression models (Agresti, 1990, pp. 79-119) are estimated. The logits of the first model correspond to the binary variable of whether the individual has or has not experienced circular migration to the U.S. Similarly, the logits of the second model are related to the individual's experience of circular migration to any country in general. Therefore, the estimation of these logistic regression models will suggest the characteristics of the individuals or of those aspects of their environment that influence their likelihood of circular migration. The independent variables utilize the information gathered in the sample described above in order to test hypotheses 1 to 4 shown in the previous section.

Hypothesis 1 is operationalized by using dummies for unemployment (1 if the person is unemployed, 0 otherwise), landlessness (1 if the individual owns land, 0 otherwise), seasonal wage work (1 if the person is a seasonal wage worker, 0 otherwise), and rural wage work (1 if the person is a rural wage worker, 0 otherwise). Additionally, a group of eight dummy variables have been included to control for individual's occupation, taking subsistence peasants as the baseline for comparison. These dummies are coded as one if the person's occupation is indicated, and zero otherwise. The occupational dummies are the following: informal sector, retired, managerial or professional, technical or administrative support, service (including household), manufacturing, crafts or arts, and armed forces. Other personal characteristics have been included: number of years of education completed, gender (1 if female, 0 otherwise), number of children the person interviewed has, age of individual, student status (1 if the individual is a student, 0 otherwise), house ownership (1 if owner, 0 otherwise), land renter (1 if the person rents land, 0 otherwise), land ownership (1 if owner, 0 otherwise), internal migration experience (1 if the person has migrated ever within the country, 0 otherwise), and marital status. The operationalization of internal migration experience is done by asking the respondents if they were born in the area where they currently live or somewhere else in the country, since all the interviewees were born in El Salvador. Five dummies are used to operationalize marital status, keeping singles as the baseline for comparison: married, divorced, separated, lives with someone, and widow(er). In each case, the fulfillment of such a marital status is indicated by one, and zero otherwise.

In order to test hypothesis 2, three types of networks are operationalized: religious network affiliation, networks of relatives in the U.S., and Salvadoran community networks. Thus, taking non-religious affiliation as the baseline group, three other religious group affiliations are operationalized by dummy variables: Catholics, Evangelists, and other religious affiliation. In each case, one indicates affiliation and zero the opposite. In addition, another dummy variable indicates if the individual has a support network of relatives living in the U.S. (1 if has relatives, 0 otherwise). Finally, one more dummy variable shows if the person is related to community organizations (1 if related, 0 otherwise).

Hypothesis 3 is operationalized by three dummy variables; the first dummy indicates if the person supports the Farabundo Martí National Liberation Front (FMLN) (1 if does, 0 otherwise); the second dummy shows if the individual is a union member (1 if the person is unionized, 0 otherwise); and the third dummy reveals if the interviewee has experienced a death in the family due to the civil war (1 if such a death occurred, 0 otherwise).

Finally, hypothesis 4 is operationalized by thirteen dummy variables, using the Ahuachapán department as the baseline for comparison. These dummies indicate the department of residence of the person interviewed (1 if the person resides in such a department, 0 otherwise). One dummy variable is used for each department: Santa Ana, Cabañas, Usulután, San Miguel, Morazán, La Unión, Chalatenango, Sonsonate, La Libertad, San Salvador, La Paz, Cuscatlán, and San Vicente. The presence of the FMLN was the most prominent in the departments of Chalatenango, Morazán, Cuscatlán, San Vicente, Usulután, Guazapa, and Santa Ana, where during different periods there were temporary or well-established revolutionary local governments (Montgomery, 1995, p. 119; Moreno-Parada, 1994, pp. 110-111).

FINDINGS AND DISCUSSION

Focusing on several selected variables, Table 1 shows the percentages of circular and non-circular migrants to the U.S. from impoverished Salvadoran suburban areas. Each row of Table 1 indicates these percentages for individuals who satisfy each characteristic mentioned in the first column. The number of cases with a particular characteristic is shown in parentheses. For example, out of 351 individuals who indicate political support for the FMLN (100% of this group), 96% of them have not experienced circular migration to the U.S. and 4.0% have; also, among the 855 individuals who did not support the FMLN, 96.8% have not experienced circular migration and 3.2% have.

The results in Table 1 show that the percentage of circular migrants among those with relatives in the U.S. (15.4%) is more than three times the percentage of migrants among those without relatives in the U.S. (2.8%). Similarly, the percentage of male migrants (4.8%) is more than fifteen times the percentage of female migrants (0.3%). Furthermore, the percentage of migrants to the U.S. among those with previous migratory experience within the country (8.4%) is about four times that of the migrants without that previous experience (2.3%). There is a considerable difference between the average number of educational years of circular U.S. migrants (6.28 years) and the average education of non-circular U.S. migrants (3.74 years). Additionally, the educational median of migrants (6.0 complete years of education) is twice that of the non-migrants (3.0).

A second group of variables shows less striking percentage differences between circular migrants and non-migrants to the U.S.; the percentage of house owners with U.S. circular migratory experience (4.2%) is almost double that of those who do not own a house (2.4%); land renters (4.2% versus 3.4% of those not renting land), employed individuals (4.2% versus 3.0% of the unemployed), union members (4.5% versus 3.5% of non-unionized workers), persons not connected to community organizations (4.4% compared to 2.9% of the connected ones), and individuals with other religion (5.3% compared to 3.1% of Catholics, 96.2% of evangelists, and 4.3% of the non-religious ones). Table 1 also shows that the mean age of circular migrants (41.53) and non-migrants (42.78) only differ by approximately one year, but the median age of migrants (43.0 years) is larger than the median age of non-migrants (40.0 years) by three years. Finally, supporters of the FMLN (4.0%) do not constitute a much larger group of circular mi-

TABLE 1. Percentage of circular and non-circular migrants to the U.S. among individuals with varied characteristics. The sample is taken from Salvadoran impoverished suburban areas. Percentages for selected variables are shown (1995).

Variable	Number of Cases	Not Circular Migrants	Circular Migrants
Have relatives in the U.S.	52	84.6	15.4
No relatives in the U.S.	1121	97.2	2.8
Support the FMLN	351	96.0	4.0
Do not support the FMLN	855	96.8	3.2
Have migrated within the country	203	91.6	8.4
Have not migrated within the country	983	97.7	2.3
Females	358	99.7	0.3
Males	876	95.2	4.8
House owners	667	95.8	4.2
Not house owners	536	97.6	2.4
Land renters	236	95.8	4.2
Not land renters	979	96.6	3.4
Land owners	289	96.5	3.5
Not land owners	945	96.5	3.5
Linked to community organizations	760	97.1	2.9
Not linked to community organizations	474	95.6	4.4
Unemployed	756	97.0	3.0
Employed	478	95.8	4.2
Union members	22	95.5	4.5
Not union members	1212	96.5	3.5
Catholics	905	96.9	3.1
Evangelists	185	96.2	3.8

TABLE 1 (continued)

Variable	Number of Cases	Not Circular Migrants	Circular Migrants
Other religion	76	94.7	5.3
Not religious	47	95.7	4.3
Age mean (for all cases = 42.67)	1470	42.78	41.53
Age median (for all cases = 40.0)	1470	40.0	43.0
Mean of the number of years of education completed (all cases- 3.71)	1435	3.74	6.28
Median of the number of years of education completed (all cases = 3.0)	1435	3.0	6.0

grants than its opponents (3.2%). How significant are the former variables on the likelihood of circular migration to the U.S.? The following discussion aims to address this question.

Results from Table 2 show that Salvadorans living in impoverished suburban areas are more likely to engage in circular migration to any other country if they are educated, male, own a house, and have experienced internal migration previously to their international migration experience. In addition, Evangelists or members of other non-Catholic and non-Evangelist religions are more likely than Catholics and non-religious Salvadorans to become circular migrants. Table 2 also shows that manufacturing laborers are more likely than rural workers or peasants to be circular migrants. In contrast to the previous positive factors to migrate, being a female or having a connection to a community organization decreases the likelihood of becoming a circular migrant to another country.

Thus, the analysis of circular migrants to the U.S. indicates their share of some similarities with the migrants to other countries (Table 2). The more educated individuals are, the more likely they are to engage in circular migration to the U.S. Also, males are more prone to migrate to the U.S. than females, as well as those individuals with previous

TABLE 2. Logistic Regression Model for Salvadoran Circular Migration (1995). Model 1 refers to circular migration to any country from El Salvador's impoverished suburban areas. Model 2 refers to circular migration to the U.S. from El Salvador's impoverished suburban areas.

Variable	Model 1		Model 2	
	Parameter Estimate (Standard Error)		Parameter Estimate (Standard Error)	
Education	0.18**	(0.05)	0.39**	(0.12)
Female	−1.79**	(0.51)	−5.42**	(1.88)
Number of Kids	−0.01	(0.07)	−0.13	(0.18)
Age	0.02	(0.01)	0.03	(0.03)
Student	0.35	(0.67)	−1.11	(1.73)
House owner	0.37**	(0.18)	−1.19*	(0.80)
Land owner	−0.09	(0.37)	0.49	(0.74)
Rents land	−0.56	(0.41)	−1.60*	(0.88)
Seasonal worker	0.17	(0.34)	−0.59	(0.77)
Rural worker	−0.42	(0.59)	−8.35	(73.44)
Union member	0.72	(0.74)	−11.32	(151.34)
Unemployed	0.15	(0.43)	0.09	(0.82)
Membership in community organization(s)	−0.67**	(0.31)	−2.23**	(0.79)
Has relatives in the U.S.	1.35	(0.50)	2.57**	(0.89)
Has experienced internal migration within the country	0.90**	(0.36)	1.71**	(0.79)
Experienced a death in the family due to the civil war	−0.02	(0.09)	−0.17	(0.23)
Supports the FMLN	−0.11	(0.35)	0.33	(0.70)
Department of Residence				
Santa Ana	−0.83	(0.76)	10.56	(59.22)
Cabañas	0.10	(0.62)	9.30	(59.21)
Usulután	−1.49	(1.15)	−0.55	(108.81)
San Miguel	0.06	(0.66)	10.91	(59.22)
Morazán	−0.93	(0.88)	7.90	(59.24)

TABLE 2 (continued)

Variable	Model 1		Model 2	
	Parameter Estimate (Standard Error)		Parameter Estimate (Standard Error)	
La Unión	0.83	(0.66)	11.37	(59.22)
Chalatenango	0.81	(0.59)	10.10	(59.21)
Sonsonate	0.24	(0.66)	7.96	(59.23)
La Libertad	−0.33	(0.76)	−0.28	(104.25)
San Salvador	−0.75	(0.76)	7.80	(59.22)
LaPaz	−1.15	(1.14)	−0.46	(125.81)
Cuscatlán	−0.52	(0.68)	−1.50	(92.68)
San Vicente	0.61	(0.63)	11.47	(59.22)
Religion				
Catholic	1.39	(1.11)	10.76	(85.80)
Evangelist	1.85*	(1.14)	10.72	(85.80)
Other religion	2.33**	(1.17)	10.36	(85.80)
Marital Status				
Married	−0.04	(0.43)	−1.20	(0.99)
Divorced	0.42	(1.38)	−11.90	(248.72)
Separated	0.68	(0.93)	−10.76	(117.25)
Lives with someone	0.40	(0.43)	0.48	(0.93)
Widow(er)	1.00	(0.72)	−0.86	(1.77)
Occupation				
Informal sector	0.17	(0.47)	1.03	(1.00)
Retired	−0.43	(1.28)	−6.94	(232.90)
Managerial or professional	0.04	(1.21)	−11.51	(249.15)
Technical or administrative support	−0.17	(0.59)	−0.48	(1.22)
Service, including household	0.12	(0.79)	−0.78	(1.60)
Manufacturing laborer	2.15*	(1.13)	−6.96	(256.71)
Crafts or arts	−5.04	(13.80)	−8.36	(220.73)
Armed forces	−5.48	(36.67)	−11.13	(736.20)
Intercept	−4.75**	(1.64)	−20.80	(104.30)
N = 1,487	G-squared = 89.63; df = 6		G-squared = 96.58; df = 46	

*p < .14   Goodness of fit = 765.19   Goodness of fit = 528.66

**p < .05

internal migration experience. Finally, participation in community organizations decreases the likelihood of circular migration to the U.S. as it does to any other country. However, Model 2 in Table 2 also indicates some differences between circular migrants to the U.S. and circular migrants in general.

First, house ownership or renting land decreases the likelihood of circular migration to the U.S., although it does the opposite in the case of other countries, indicating that perhaps migrating to other Central American countries could be shorter or less cumbersome than migrating to the U.S. Table 3 shows that the highest percentage of circular migrants go to other Central American countries (55.8%) with the U.S. in second place (38%), followed by other Latin American countries outside Central America (5.3%), and all other countries at the end (0.9%). Table 3 also shows that the majority of circular migrants that come to the U.S. do not migrate to México first, they seem to come directly to the U.S., although this may require passing through the Mexican territory.

Second, to have relatives in the U.S. increases the probability of migrating to the U.S., but it does not affect the odds of doing so to other countries. Therefore, relatives in the U.S. may be more likely to be resources for migrants to travel to the U.S. but not to other countries. A third important difference between circular migrants to the

TABLE 3. Percentages of Salvadoran circular migration from impoverished suburban areas to other regions (1995).

Region or Country	Percentage
A Central American country other than El Salvador	55.8
A Latin American country other than Central America	5.3
Other	0.9
United States	34.5
Mexico and the U.S.	3.5
Total to the U.S.	38.0

U.S. and other countries is that religion is not a relevant factor in moving to the U.S. Thus, religious networks seem to be significant resources in moving to other countries–especially in Central America–than in moving to the U.S. Finally, although being a manufacturer worker increases the likelihood of circular migration to other countries, it is not significant in the case of migration to the U.S. Hence, across occupations, the likelihood of migrating to the U.S. for impoverished suburban Salvadoran people is the same according to Model 2 (Table 2).

The non-significant parameters in both models in Table 2 are also very informative for our analysis. In the first place, support for the FMLN does not constitute a significant reason to engage in circular migration, nor does having experienced the death of a relative during the civil war. Analogously, union membership does not increase the likelihood of becoming circular migrants. Consequently, it seems that politics is not a relevant reason to influence the decision to become a circular migrant. Therefore, according to our results, circular migrants from disadvantaged suburban Salvadoran areas are not likely to be political refugees.

Second, there are no significant differences among individuals from different Salvadoran departments to participate in circular migration. This may be a consequence of the relative small size of the country, which allows individuals from all regions to migrate equally, without allowing those living closer to the borders to have a significant advantage. Additionally, this may indicate further support for the former results indicating a lack of political motivation to become circular migrants. As our results show, Salvadorans from departments known to have been very supportive of the FMLN during the civil war, namely Chalatenango, Morazán, La Unión, and Sonsonate, among others (Wickham-Crowley, 1992, pp. 243-244), are equally likely as people from other departments not very supportive of the revolutionaries–such as Ahuachapán, Cuscatlán, and others–to engage in circular migration.

Third, age and marital status do not affect the chances of circular migration, nor does being unemployed. Thus, Salvadoran circular migrants from impoverished suburban areas do not follow the traditional pattern of migrants in general, who tend to be employed but looking for a better paid job (Portes and Rumbaut, 1996, pp. 14-27).

Finally, the population in this study who lives off the land, such as land owners, land renters, seasonal workers, and rural workers in general, are no different from their Salvadoran counterparts to experience circular migration. Hence, if indeed rural workers and peasants have formed a significant constituency of leftist and center-leftist political movements in El Salvador (Wickham-Crowley, 1992; LaFeber, 1993), our results may indicate that such political involvement does not increase the likelihood of becoming circular migrants.

In view of the outcomes obtained, hypothesis 1 is not supported by the results concerning unemployment or underemployment (including seasonal workers, rural workers, and employees in the informal, service, and crafts sectors). Contrary to hypothesis 1, our results indicate that more educated people–less burdened by illiteracy–are more likely to migrate than their less educated counterparts. However, hypothesis 1 receives some support as well; house owners and land renters are less likely to become circular migrants to the U.S. than those without these resources, although the opposite holds for migrants to other countries in the case of house owners. This situation may indicate that house owners can allocate resources to other activities that otherwise would be spent paying house rent. Additionally, periodic or continuous house maintenance is possible if the owners migrate to neighboring Central American countries whereas U.S. migration may be longer, more expensive, and require the sale of the property.

As our results indicate above, hypothesis 2 is strongly sustained. Individuals with a support network of relatives living in the U.S. are more likely to migrate to that country than those without such a network resource. Additionally, links to networks in the sending country, such as community organizations, decrease the probability of migrating to the U.S. or to any other country. Religious networks, as indicated by membership in Evangelist, or in non-Catholic and non-Evangelist churches, increase the likelihood of being circular migrants to other countries except the U.S. vis-à-vis non-religious or Catholic individuals. In the case of the U.S. migrants, these religious networks do not make a significant difference.

Contrary to hypothesis 3, our results indicate that supporters of the FMLN, unionized workers, the members of the armed forces, or those individuals who experienced a family loss during the civil war are as likely as their counterparts to become involved in circular migration–to the U.S. or any other country. Thus, circular migrants from El

Salvador's impoverished suburban areas do not seem to be significantly influenced by political reasons.

Analogously, hypothesis 4 is not supported by our tests. Individuals from all Salvadoran impoverished suburban areas across the country have the same likelihood to be circular migrants to the U.S. or to any other region.

CONCLUSIONS

This study has tested the relevance of individual and structural theories of migration for Salvadoran circular migrants to the U.S. and other countries. Using 1995 individual data taken from impoverished suburban areas corresponding to cities across the fourteen Salvadoran geographic departments, our results strongly support the relevance of network theories of migration. In the first place, networks of relatives in the U.S. increase the likelihood of becoming circular migrants among the members of the sample. Second, attachments to local networks decrease the probability of joining the migration flow to any country. Third, religious membership does not influence the chances of migrating to the U.S., although Evangelists and other non-Catholic religious groups do have a higher likelihood of circular migration to other countries. This may suggest that there is a significant amount of organized religious exchange and proselytism across several areas of Central America.

Alternatively, push-pull or cost-benefit theories of migration receive mixed support by our tests. On one hand, unemployment, seasonal and rural wage work, or working in the informal sector do not influence the likelihood to migrate to the U.S. On the other hand, Salvadoran circular migrants tend to be males, more educated than their non-migrant counterparts, less likely to migrate to the U.S. if they rent land or own a house, and with previous internal migratory experience. Similarly, marital status, age, and occupation do not influence individuals' decision to migrate to the U.S. However, manufacturing laborers do migrate more to other countries than workers in the remaining occupations.

Another central task of our study has been to test the significance of political reasons to participate in circular migration. Despite the relevance attributed to politics by several authors (de la Garza & Szekely, 1997; Portes & Rumbaut, 1996; Sassen, 1995a), Salvadoran circular migrants in our sample do not seem to be influenced by political support in favor of the FMLN, membership in unions, participation in the armed forces, nor by the experience of a family death during the civil war. Furthermore, the well-known differential distribution of political support in favor of the FMLN across the country's geographic departments (Wickham-Crowley, 1992; LaFeber, 1993) does not affect the likelihood of circular migration in our sample. Thus, individuals from Ahuachapán, a notable politically stable province, are as likely as those individuals from Chalatenango, Sonsonate, Morazán, or La Unión, former civil war strongholds of the FMLN, to become circular migrants.

Therefore, if our analysis of Salvadoran circular migrants indicates a broader pattern of migration, one may hypothesize that the wave of migration to the U.S. from El Salvador, and perhaps from Central America in general, has changed with respect to the general migration trends of previous periods. Following Hamilton and Stoltz-Chinchilla (1997, p. 89), the majority of Central American migrants arriving in the U.S. before 1975 came for economic reasons. However, by the second half of the 1970s, many were escaping violence, repression, or persecution at home, which accelerated in the mid-1970s. In the case of El Salvador, this trend lasted up to the end of the civil war and the signing of the peace treaty in 1992. Hence, based on our findings for circular or return migrants, Salvadoran migrants to the U.S. since the mid-1990s may be constituted most significantly by those individuals who are connected to the networks of Salvadorans in the U.S., formed by friends and relatives who emigrated during the previous years, and who are not likely to leave their country for political or urgent economic reasons (unemployment, underemployment, seasonal or rural wage work). In addition, these new Salvadoran migrants are likely to be more educated than their counterparts who do not migrate and to have previous internal migratory experience within or without their country. In sum, the Salvadoran migrants to the U.S. since the mid-1990s, may be economic migrants in search of better labor market opportunities in the U.S. with the help of networks already established in this country.

Finally, our study also suggests the need to follow up with a broader, more representative sample of Salvadorans, covering more extended urban and rural areas and social groups, as well as individuals living in both the sending and the receiving countries (Goldring, 1992;

Massey, 1987; Massey, Alarcon, Durand, & Gonzalez, 1987), in order to analyze the relevance of our former hypotheses to the remaining Salvadoran population. As this study has shown, the current immigration trend from Central America is based fundamentally on changing structural factors involving both the sending and the receiving communities in El Salvador and the U.S. Thus, in order to enact effective migration policy measures, policy makers have to base their analysis on accurate knowledge of the factors that compel individuals to migrate. Our study was inspired by this necessity.

REFERENCES

Agresti, A. (1990). *Categorical Data Analysis*. New York: John Wiley and Sons.

Americas Watch. (1991). *El Salvador's Decade of Terror: Human Rights since the Assassination of Archbishop Romero*. New Haven: Yale University Press.

Cordoba-Macias, R. (1996). El Salvador: Transition from Civil War. In J. I. Dominguez & A. F. Lowenthal (Eds.), *Constructing Democratic Governance: Latin America and the Caribbean in the 1990s* (pp. 26-49). Baltimore: John Hopkins University Press.

Borjas, G. J. (1990). *Friends or Strangers: The Impact of Immigrants on the U.S. Economy*. New York: Basic Books.

de la Garza, R. O., & Szekely, G.. (1997). Policy, Politics, and Emigration: Reexamining the Mexican Experience. In F. D. Bean, R. O. de la Garza, B. R. Roberts, & S. Weintraub (Eds.), *At the Crossroads: México and the U.S. Immigration Policy* (pp. 201-225). Maryland: Rowman and Littlefield.

Gelbard, A. H., & Carter, M. (1997). Mexican Immigration and the U.S. Population. In F. D. Bean, R. O. de la Garza, B. R. Roberts, & S. Weintraub (Eds.), *At the Crossroads: México and the U.S. Immigration Policy* (pp. 117-144). Maryland: Rowman and Littlefield.

Goldring, L. P. (1992). La Migración México-EUA y la Transnacionalización del Espacio Político y Social: Perspectivas desde el México Rural. *Estudios Sociológicos, 10*, 315-340.

Hamilton, N. & Stoltz-Chinchilla, N. (1997). Central American Migration: A Framework for Analysis. In M. Romero, P. Hondagneu-Sotelo, & V. Ortiz (Eds.), *Challenging Fronteras: Structuring Latina and Latino Lives in the U.S.* (pp. 81-100). New York: Routledge.

Hirschman, A. O. (1970). *Exit, Voice and Loyalty: Responses to Decline in Firms, Organizations and States*. Cambridge: Harvard University Press.

Granovetter, M. (1995). The Economic Sociology of Firms and Entrepreneurs. In A. Portes (Ed.), *The Economic Sociology of Immigration: Essays on Networks, Ethnicity, and Entrepreneurship*. New York: Russell Sage Foundation.

LaFeber, W. (1993). *Inevitable Revolutions: The United States in Central America*. New York: W.W. Norton and Co.

Massey, D. S. (1987). The Ethnosurvey in Theory and Practice, *International Migration Review, 21*, 1498-1522.

Massey, D. S., Alarcon, R., Durand, J., & Gonzalez, II. (1987). *Return to Aztlán: The Social Process of International Migration from Western México*. California: University of California Press.

Masud-Piloto, F. (1996). *From Welcomed Exiles to Illegal Immigrants: Cuban Migration to the U.S., 1959-1995*. Maryland: Rowman and Littlefield.

Montgomery, T. S. (1995). *Revolution in El Salvador: From Civil Strife to Civil Peace*. Second Edition. Boulder: Westview Press.

Moreno-Parada, F. (1994). *El Salvador: La Sociedad contra El Estado*. Jalisco: Universidad de Guadalajara Press.

Portes, A. (1995). Children of Immigrants: Segmented Assimilation and Its Determinants. In A. Portes (Ed.), *The Economic Sociology of Immigration: Essays on Networks, Ethnicity, and Entrepreneurship* (pp. 248-280). New York: Russell Sage.

Portes, A., & Rumbaut, R. C. (1996). *Immigrant America: A Portrait*. Second Edition. California: University of California.

Roberts, B. R., & Escobar-Latapi, A. (1997). Mexican Social and Economic Policy and Emigration. In F. D. Bean, R. O. de la Garza, B. R. Roberts, & S. Weintraub (Eds.), *At the Crossroads: México and the U.S. Immigration Policy* (pp. 47-78). Maryland: Rowman and Littlefield.

Ruggles, P., & Fix, M. (1985). *Impacts and Potential Impacts of Central American Migrants on HHS and Related Programs of Assistance: Final Report*. Washington, D.C.: Urban Institute.

Sassen, S. (1995a). Why Migration? In F. Rosen & D. McFadyen (Eds.), *Free Trade and Economic Restructuring in Latin America: A NACLA Reader* (pp. 272-285). New York: Monthly Review.

Sassen, S. (1995b). Immigration and Local Labor Markets. In A. Portes (Ed.), *The Economic Sociology of Immigration: Essays on Networks, Ethnicity, and Entrepreneurship* (pp. 87-127). New York: Russell Sage Foundation.

Schaefer, R. T., & Lamm, R. P.. (1997). *Sociology: A Brief Introduction*. Second Edition. New York: McGraw-Hill.

Thomas, B. (1973). *Migration and Economic Growth: A Study of Great Britain and the Atlantic Economy*. Cambridge: Cambridge University Press.

U.S. General Accounting Office (GAO). (1989). *Central America: Conditions of Refugees and Displaced Persons*. Washington, D.C.: Government Printing Office.

Weintraub, S. (1997). U.S. Foreign Policy and Mexican Immigration. In F. D. Bean, R. O. de la Garza, B. R. Roberts, & S. Weintraub (Eds.), *At the Crossroads: México and the U.S. Immigration Policy* (pp. 284-298). Maryland: Rowman and Littlefield.

Wickham-Crowley, T. P. (1992). *Guerrillas and Revolution in Latin America: A Comparative Study of Insurgents and Regimes Since 1956*. New Jersey: Princeton University Press.

APPENDIX

Population in Salvadoran departments and municipalities containing the areas in the sample (1995).

Department	Population	Municipality	Population
Ahuachapán	289,047	Ahuachapán	95,540
Cabañas	148,302	Ilobasco	58,206
Chalatenango	190,040	Chalatenango	29,474
Cuscatlán	192,119	Cojutepeque	48,908
La Libertad	584,971	La Libertad	38,217
La Paz	269,244	Zacatecoluca	61,533
La Unión	274,581	Santa Rosa de Lima	26,343
Morazán	169,319	San Francisco Gotera	20,209
San Miguel	440,722	San Miguel	212,067
San Salvador	1,724,517	San Salvador	445,614
San Salvador Metropolitan Area	1,697,023		
San Vicente	152,236	San Vicente	48,235
Santa Ana	503,997	Santa Ana	230,423
Sonsonate	399,854	Sonsonate	86,280
Usulután	329,656	Usulután	67,109
Total	5,668,605		

Pilsen and The Resurrection Project: Community Organization in a Latino Community

Susan F. Grossman
Rita M. Cardoso
Giselle G. Belanger
Jerry Belski
Tyra C. Corethers
Mary E. Pettinelli
Maurice A. Redd

SUMARY. This article describes a Latino community on the near southwest side of Chicago and the attempts of a community-based organization to respond to community issues and concerns. We first describe the history and characteristics of the community, highlight some of the challenges it currently faces and then discuss the development and activities of a unique church-based community organization. The organizing effort is assessed in light of the literature on community intervention as well as in relation to the community's cultural heritage and

---

Susan F. Grossman, PhD, Rita M. Cardoso, BSW, Giselle G. Belanger, MSN, Jerry Belski, MSW, Tyra C. Corethers, MSW, Mary E. Pettinelli, MSW, and Maurice A. Redd, BA, are all affiliated with Loyola University-Chicago, School of Social Work.

Address correspondence, questions and comments to: Susan F. Grossman, PhD, Assistant Professor, Loyola University, Chicago, School of Social Work, 820 N. Michigan Avenue, Chicago, IL 60611 (e-mail: sgrossm@luc.edu).

The authors wish to thank Dr. Maria Vidal de Haymes for her thoughtful comments and feedback and Amanda Whitlock and Angela Thies-Huber for their assistance and insights.

[Haworth co-indexing entry note]: "Pilsen and The Resurrection Project: Community Organization in a Latino Community." Grossman, Susan F. et al. Co-published simultaneously in *Journal of Poverty* (The Haworth Press, Inc.) Vol. 4, No. 1/2, 2000, pp. 131-149; and: *Latino Poverty in the New Century: Inequalities, Challenges and Barriers* (ed: Maria Vidal de Haymes, Keith M. Kilty, and Elizabeth A. Segal) The Haworth Press, Inc., 2000, pp. 131-149. Single or multiple copies of this article are available for a fee from The Haworth Document Delivery Service [1-800-342-9678, 9:00 a.m. - 5:00 p.m. (EST). E-mail address: getinfo@haworthpressinc.com].

characteristics. *[Article copies available for a fee from The Haworth Document Delivery Service: 1-800-342-9678. E-mail address: <getinfo@haworthpressinc. com> Website: <http://www.haworthpressinc.com>]*

KEYWORDS. Latinos, poverty, community organizing, community development

Definitions of community typically include two distinct viewpoints, one emphasizing locality as the basis of community identification and a second focusing on shared interests, ties or belief systems (Fellin, 1995; Brueggmann, 1996). These two foci need not be mutually exclusive. Shared interests may be based on common geographic boundaries as well as other factors such as religious or racial solidarity. Yet, increasingly, locality based communities may find themselves comprised of a number of smaller "communities of meaning" which may not always agree on or benefit equally from community action. Community organizing strategies may need to vary, depending on the organizational constituency and the extent to which it is (or desires to be) integrated into the larger locality. Using Rothman's (1979) model of community organizing strategies, we can speculate that the more conflictual the situation, the more social action approaches will make sense as opposed to community or locality development models.

At the same time, Rivera and Erlich (1998) suggest that for communities of meaning based on racial or cultural solidarity, the usual models of community organizing, i.e., locality development, social planning and social action, cannot be uniformly applied. They argue that racial and cultural identity more than locale, may be the issue of paramount importance in organizing efforts, and they maintain that such identification has profound implications for the economic and political configuration of each community (Rivera and Erlich, 1998). They also claim that racial and cultural identity are integral factors in the process of empowerment and the development of critical consciousness (Rivera and Erlich, 1998, p. 10). Organizers need to be aware of the racial, ethnic and cultural uniqueness of people of color and the implications of these unique qualities in relation to such critical variables as kinship patterns, social systems, the way in which power is viewed, and leadership networks that develop (Rivera and Erlich, 1998).

Mexican-American communities have a long and rich history of community organization in the United States, beginning as far back as

1894 with the creation of Alianza Hispano Americana, the first successful organization for Mexican American rights which helped to combat racism and discrimination faced by Mexican Americans living in the southwest (Montiel and Ortega y Gasca, 1998).

Nonetheless, Dahm and Harper (1999) identify a number of religious and social norms that tend to prevent many Mexican people who are coming to the United States from effectively organizing for justice. These include the belief that suffering is good, that life on earth is a time of trial in preparation for the next life in heaven, that politics is evil, and that life in the United States is far better than life in Mexico, even if the housing is poor, the jobs are low paying, city government is neglectful and the schools are crowded (Dahm and Harper, p. 170). Further, Dahm and Harper (1999) point out that as a result of centuries of oppression, many Mexican Americans feel that they have no power to make a difference.

This article describes a Mexican-American community located on the near Southwest side of Chicago and the history and efforts of one community organization to empower its residents. The community is one in which community identification is based on both shared locale and shared meanings, primarily in the form of a common ethnic identity. The organization described reflects the cultural uniqueness of community residents, preserving and adapting indigenous networks and culturally relevant sources of support and power, as well as employing traditional organizing efforts to bring about change.

THE COMMUNITY

The Pilsen community is located in what is known as Chicago's "Lower West Side." It is surrounded by current and former industrial areas, and is situated about one and a half miles from Chicago's downtown or "Loop" area (Baker, 1995). Together with two adjacent communities, Heart of Chicago and Little Village, it serves as a center for Chicago's flourishing Mexican community, and, along with these other two communities, it continues to be a "port of entry" for Spanish-speaking families (Pacyga and Skerrett, 1986).

Data from the 1990 census indicate that approximately 46,000 people live in the community and almost all (88%) are Latino, primarily individuals of Mexican descent (Conrad and Cooksey, 1997). The impact and influence of Mexican immigrants on Pilsen is obvious. The tremendous conservation of the Mexican culture, religion, traditions, Spanish language, and traditional dishes, make Pilsen feel like a "Mexican Village." This is evident in the numerous Mexican restaurants, Spanish storefronts and billboards as well as in the colorful murals on sides of buildings which depict Mexican history and beliefs. Indeed, in the heart of Pilsen, there is a new monument honoring and recognizing the richness of the Mexican culture and its significance to the community.

The effects of the low income level of the community are also evident. A recent study, conducted by the University of Illinois Voorhees Center for Neighborhood and Community Improvement (1995a), indicates that of the 12,340 households in the community, 35% make less than $15,000 a year. Median income is $20,571, almost $6000 less than the median income for the city ($26,301), and only 8.4% of all households make over $50,000 a year (University of Illinois, 1995a). In 1990, 28% of Pilsen's residents were below the poverty level; 16% received some type of public assistance (Conrad and Cooksey, 1997).

Two-thirds of Pilsen residents rent housing (University of Illinois, 1995a), yet only 22% of the community's housing units are owner-occupied (Conrad and Cooksey, 1997). This compares to a citywide average of nearly 40% (Conrad and Cooksey, 1997). The majority of homeowners do not live in the community. Not surprisingly, in some sections of Pilsen, homes are obviously in need of repair and are poorly maintained. Litter covers the streets and sanitation problems are reported by local residents (Lutton, 1998).

Dilapidated housing is a major problem and many of the houses are very old. Almost 80% of Pilsen's housing stock was built prior to 1940 (Conrad and Cooksey, 1997). Further, conditions in the parts of the community that have not been undergoing gentrification are crowded; 1990 census data indicate that occupancy rates in the community average 3.7 people per room (Lutton, 1998). Yet, because of its affordability (average rent and utilities, according to a 1995 study by the Voorhees Center, are only $448 per month; University of Illinois, 1995b), and its strong connection with Mexican culture, Pilsen remains a desirable community for many of its residents.

History and Political Activity

The Chicago neighborhood of Pilsen has a rich history of struggle to preserve a sense of community and justice for its working-class and immigrant inhabitants. In the 1860s, the construction of a series of bridges and tunnels made the community more accessible to many working class people. For the next few decades, a large number of groups lived in Pilsen and then relocated. Adelman (1983) estimates, in fact, that over 26 ethnic groups inhabited this diverse community at some time.

Mexican-American workers began moving into the community in the 1920s. According to Adelman (1983), these were individuals who worked for the railroad and for International Harvester, both of which were in close proximity to the community. Nonetheless, up until 1960, Pilsen was still a "relatively self-sufficient enclave of Eastern European immigrants, with a retail strip, seven thriving Catholic parishes and a riverside manufacturing district with plentiful low-skill jobs" (Lanier, 1988, p. 17; see also Baker, 1995). After 1960, the Mexican population grew rapidly, and by 1979, Pilsen had become the second largest community of Mexican-American people in the United States (Adelman, 1983).

Due to the location of the neighborhood, it has had a push and pull relationship with the wealthy and elite since the mid-1800s. As discussed subsequently, this struggle continues with the neighborhood's current Mexican-American population.

As a variety of immigrant groups moved into and out of this area, many of them participated in significant events of America's labor movement. For example, in 1886, 80,000 Chicagoans, a majority of whom were from Pilsen and Westside neighborhoods, protested on Michigan Avenue to support the national campaign for an eight-hour working day. Two days later, dozens of workers from the McCormick Reaper Plant were wounded and one was killed. This event triggered a meeting of workers at Haymarket Square and the Haymarket bombing and riot (Adelman, 1983). Similarly, the Garment Workers' Strike of 1910 started at a Hart, Schaffner and Marx manufacturing shop in Pilsen and eventually led to the creation of the Amalgamated Clothing Workers of America (Pacyga and Skerrett, 1986).

In light of its history of housing poor and working class families, Pilsen was also one of the communities initially targeted by the Settlement House movement of Jane Addams. The tradition of political organizing, social service development, community and cultural preservation fostered by the Settlement House movement was embraced by the largely Latino neighborhood in the 1960s and 1970s as residents fought to establish control of their community. A number of community organizations, including Pilsen Neighbors Community Council, ALLAS, Casa Aztlan, the 18th Street Development Corporation, El Hogar del Nino (a child care cooperative), and El Centro de la Causa (a community youth center) were established; many still exist today (Lanier, 1988; Conrad and Cooksey, 1997; Adelman, 1983; Baker, 1995). There was strong community involvement in the development of Benito-Juarez High School in the 1970s (Adelman, 1983) and there have been medical centers and social service agencies developed, as well as coalitions to fight issues related to housing and local business interests.

Historically, Pilsen has been represented by an Italian alderman and was part of a ward that included a larger Italian neighborhood. Redistricting and migration into the Italian community in the 1980s changed this. Both Pilsen and Heart of Chicago were combined into a largely Latino district and a Latino Alderman from the community was elected to City Council. However, the new ward included other ethnic communities, particularly Chinatown, which has made organizing the ward on behalf of Latino interests more challenging.

Cultural preservation efforts in the 1960s and 1970s included the painting of murals on the buildings of the barrio by local artists. Many of these murals are still seen throughout the neighborhood. Contemporary artist Marcos Raya noted in a 1995 interview that painting a mural involves the artist with the whole community (Lauerman, 1995). The painters often serve as role models, organizing mural projects and seeking the help of young people to paint them (Lauerman, 1995, p. 7). Further, community leaders see the cultural movement as critical to efforts for community power (Baker, 1995). In the words of one community leader, "[I]f there was no cultural movement in the neighborhood, none of the other accomplishments could have occurred" (Baker, 1995, citing Arturo Vazquez, p. 176).

Other art forms are also present in Pilsen. In 1995, Lauerman reported that three theater groups were forming. There is a center for artists, poetry reading, and political debates (Kurson, 1996). The Mexican Fine Arts Center Museum, which opened in 1987, features Latin-American artists and sponsors a speaker series (Kurson, 1996).

Religion

The church has been central to many of the community's organizing efforts (Lanier, 1988) and was a driving force behind the creation of the Resurrection Project. There are 25 churches in the community, nine of which are Catholic (Conrad and Cooksey, 1997). As Conrad and Cooksey (1997) note, religion has an important place in the lives of Pilsen's residents (p. 31). It may be the one institution that newly arrived immigrants can trust, especially if they are undocumented individuals. They know that the Church is not going to "turn them in"; rather, it will provide assistance and support.

Saint Procopius is a typical Pilsen parish. The church was established as a Benedictine Abbey in 1894, and was the first Catholic Church in Pilsen. By 1892, St. Procopius had become the largest Bohemian parish in the United States, and in 1897 was canonically appointed the administrative center for all Bohemian parishes in the United States (Adelman, 1983, p. 59). By 1963, many Mexican families were already moving into Pilsen and participating in St. Procopius Parish. A shrine to Our Lady of Guadalupe (the Patroness of the Americas) was erected in the church in 1963, and a Spanish Mass was added. By 1975, the 100th anniversary of St. Procopius, the church had become predominantly a Mexican parish and remains so today.

Education and Employment

Pilsen has only one public high school, Benito-Juarez High School. While there was strong community involvement in securing a high school for the community (Adelman, 1983), the drop-out rate, lower in more recent years, has been as high as 50% (University of Illinois, 1995a). Further, only about two-thirds or 68% of all students enrolled in the ninth grade in 1993 actually graduated in 1997 (Chicago Board of Education, 1997). Several alternative high school programs exist, including a Jesuit run Catholic High School, "Cristo Rey," which opened in September 1996. Cristo Rey has a bilingual program and utilizes a corporate internship program to help expose community youth to the corporate world, provide them with employment experience, and also help families cover the cost of tuition. Although the school is growing, however, it is still small in terms of enrollment, with a current total of 260 students (George, 1998).

Pilsen is rich with local stores and restaurants, many of which have been owned and operated by the same family for generations. According to Conrad and Cooksey (1997) almost half of Pilsen's workers are employed at industrial companies as operators, fabricators, and laborers or in precision production, craft and repair (p. 23). Another 18%

are employed in technical sales or in administrative support positions; 16% have service occupations (Conrad and Cooksey, 1997). A study by the Voorhees Center (University of Illinois, 1995a) notes that unemployment and underemployment are widespread in the community, especially among youth. And while there is a need for land for recreational purposes within the community, many of the vacant properties exist in industrial areas which need to be preserved for purposes of job production (University of Illinois, 1995a).

Community Challenges

Despite its strengths, Pilsen and its residents are challenged by a number of community problems. Some of the most pressing are presented below.

Pilsen has one of the highest rates of gang violence among Latino gangs in the city of Chicago (Gartland, 1998; also, see Illinois Criminal Justice Information Authority, 1996, p. 14; Spergel and Grossman, 1996). Exacerbating the problem is that parents and youth often live in different worlds. For example, Father James Gartland, the pastor at St. Procopius church, reports that 28 percent of the Pilsen population speak only Spanish, 13% speak only English and 59% speak both languages to varying degrees (Gartland, 1996, p. 4). Children are often the ones who are bilingual, serving as translators for their parents. Parents, in turn, may feel cut off from their children's world because of the language barrier. Or there may be tension because parents may want their children, who are assimilating and acculturating into American society, to maintain their ethnic identities (Conrad and Cooksey, 1997).

Pilsen is also a somewhat transient community. The neighborhood experiences a considerable turnover, as families look for better housing, better education, and safety for their children. Like past immigrant groups, most move westward, to the suburban areas west of Chicago. They still maintain their ties to the community through the church, however. For example, Father Gartland reports that 300 families who maintain regular church attendance no longer live in Pilsen (Gartland, 1996).

The implications of limited home ownership have become increasingly evident as urban expansion and gentrification of the areas surrounding Pilsen have occurred over the last two decades.

In 1968, the University of Illinois built its Chicago campus close to the northern border of the Pilsen community. Almost twenty years later, in the mid-1980s, development of the area directly east of Pilsen began as Dearborn Park, a middle- and upper-middle-class development located just south of Chicago's central business district or "Loop" started to spread south. Perhaps as a consequence, rent in the east side of Pilsen, which had been developed by artists looking for affordable homes and studio space, is double that of the rest of the area (Lauerman, 1995; Lutton, 1998). Similarly, property values in this section have increased 289% between 1989 and 1994; property taxes have increased as well (Lutton, 1998).

Currently, the University of Illinois is planning to expand south toward the Pilsen community. The only thing separating Pilsen from the new $125,000 to $350,000 homes will be a viaduct. An impact analysis of this expansion plan indicates that the expansion, while not the sole cause of gentrification, has the possibility of drastically speeding up the process and unleashing speculators and other market forces that will lead to the displacement of low-income residents (University of Illinois, 1995a; Lutton, 1998; Ritter, 1997).

A second threat also relates to designation of parts of the Pilsen community as a low-income Tax Increment Financing (TIF) district. The Tax Increment Financing District program is a City of Chicago program, developed pursuant to state legislation, used to eliminate blighting conditions found to be present in industrial, commercial and residential areas of the city. The program allows the city to provide financial incentives to stimulate private investment in a designated area (a TIF district) in order to remove the blighting conditions that have made it difficult to attract new development in a particular area. Tax revenues generated by TIF districts can also be used from one district to another district. Sections of Pilsen were recently approved by the Chicago City Council as a TIF district. The redevelopment area includes more than 100 vacant acres of land and 10 vacant buildings, and the city says that it will generate up to 4100 new jobs (Schultz, 1998; Lutton, 1998). Residents of Pilsen believe the TIF would mean an automatic increase in their property taxes. Community leaders contend that Pilsen residents should be part of any TIF planning to guard against displacement. Residents also question who will get the new jobs the redevelopment will supposedly create (Schultz, 1998; Lutton, 1998).

THE RESURRECTION PROJECT

History and Mission

The Resurrection Project (TRP) was initiated in 1994 by a coalition of Pilsen churches representing parishioners from the community. Historically, parishioners first became involved in organizing efforts through their involvement with Pilsen Neighbors Community Council (PNCC), a community organization formed in the 1960s to "obtain greater accountability from government and business institutions for the common good of the community" (Dahm and Harper, 1999, p. 171). According to Father Charles Dahm, pastor at St. Pius V Roman Catholic Church in Pilsen, and Nile Harper (1999), PNCC worked with churches and other community organizations to identify and train local leaders, identify common issues of concern and organize community groups to gain the social and political power needed to address community issues (p. 171). Churches, including St. Pius V, supported this movement in different degrees, but according to Father Dahm, discontent with the PNCC grew over time, among the pastors of the seven participating Catholic parishes (Dahm and Harper, 1999, p. 173). He notes that they came to feel that the paid professional staff were setting the organizing agenda and that the core leadership had lost meaningful contact with the institutional base in the churches; mass membership was also believed to be neglected and uninvolved. Further, the organization, as a result of developing independent sources of funding, had become less responsive to the interests and guidance of the member churches (Dahm and Harper, 1999, p. 173).

In response to these problems, in 1988, six Catholic parishes in Pilsen hired a professional organizer who had worked briefly with the PNCC (Dahm and Harper, 1999). Eventually, in consultation with the pastors, as well as church members and community leaders, he formed a new organization called the Catholic Community of Pilsen (CCP; Dahm and Harper, 1999, p. 174). Church involvement in the new organization was facilitated via the Board of Directors; each church identified two of its members to serve on the CCP Board. Initial organizing efforts focused on problems related to housing, gangs and community cleanup (Dahm and Harper, 1999, p. 174). Father Dahm notes that the new organization worked closely with the churches and pastors to develop an informed, broad base of participants (Dahm and Harper, 1999, p. 174). A critical component was a series of training classes that were developed and offered to a wide range of church participants, focusing on "the prophetic teaching of Jesus, the role of the church in seeking justice, and the importance of building people power for justice" (Dahm and Harper, 1999, pp. 174-175).

The Resurrection Project finally emerged in 1994 when the CCP joined with the Pilsen Resurrection Development Corporation, another church-based organization that was involved in developing low-income housing for community residents (Dahm and Harper, 1999). The two organizations had been working closely together since their inceptions and when the Executive Director of one announced that he was leaving, board members, some of whom were also involved with the other, decided the two organizations should become one. Dahm and Harper (1999) note that the "Board of Directors for the new organization reflected the base of support in the six local Catholic parishes in Pilsen . . ." (p. 175). Indeed, parish members were the initial source of the organization's constituency and power (Dahm and Harper, 1999).

To a large extent, The Resurrection Project's mission reflects its heritage. According to official organizational documents, TRP's mission is to build relationships and challenge people to act on their faith and values in order to create a healthy community through organizing, education and community development (The Resurrection Project, 1989).

Organizational Structure

At present, TRP has expanded to include eight community churches as well as representatives from community organizations and businesses. Depending on the size of their institution, they may have Board representation of two, three or four members. The organizational by-laws require that two-thirds of the Board of Directors be comprised of community residents from these various organizations and institutions, presumably as a measure to preserve the community base of the organization. In addition, the Board has a provision for a certain number of members-at-large who represent financial and community institutions outside of Pilsen.

Central to the operation of TRP's program divisions and the organization as a whole is a committee structure which allows for broad representation, not just by organizational members but by community members as well. Again, such measures seem to reflect attempts to prevent the organization from losing touch with its constituency and promoting their input. In addition to the usual administrative committees (i.e., Executive, Finance, Personnel and Resource Development), there are a number of program committees which "deal with budgets, planning, implementation, and evaluation of specific projects and initiatives related to TRP's program divisions" (The Resurrection Project, 1998b). The program committees are comprised of Board members as well as community residents, program participants and representatives from other institutions both in the community and at large.

Along with staff, program committee members set program direction. They are involved in hiring decisions related to new staff in their respective program areas and also take part in fund raising and budget activities. They get involved in accountability meetings with elected officials when necessary and initiate connections with service providers when such linkages are needed for securing services. Program committee members also take part in outreach to different community areas in order to recruit new members to the Resurrection Project. Thus, program committee representatives play an integral part in all aspects of program development and organizational operation.

Programs

The Resurrection Project has four major program divisions operating in Pilsen, Heart of Chicago, Little Village and Back of the Yards (another adjacent Mexican-American community). The foci of these divisions reflect issues and concerns that are both historic and more recent as well as of primary relevance to organizational participants. They also reflect TRP's organizational heritage.

The first program area, community organizing, focuses on building institutional power and developing new leaders from among its constituent member agencies who can be effective advocates both at the local community and metropolitan levels. Given the organization's roots in community efforts to develop, nurture and promote local leadership, more than any other activity, this program area would seem essential to TRP's purpose. Efforts have focused on developing and supporting indigenous leaders from the community, helping them to identify relevant community problems and concerns and encouraging them to participate in TRP activities to address these issues. Seeking to recognize and preserve the importance of naturally occurring community and neighborhood bonds, leaders are frequently located by

TRP members through informal neighborhood or church groups. Locally, community organizing efforts have included work with the police to develop a block club network and to implement a community policing program. Voter registration activities have also taken place.

A second program area concerns programs for families. This focus seems to be critical to the organization's continued relevance to its constituent members, given the importance of family in both the church and Latino culture. TRP has developed a number of programs to respond to the developmental needs of children, adults and families. The focus is on enhancing skills and creating opportunities which promote stronger families (The Resurrection Project, 1998a). Some of the programs for families include: Esperanza Familiar (Family Hope) which "provides a variety of faith-based, culturally sensitive courses to help families improve their communication parenting skills" (Dahm and Harper, 1999, p. 178); a second stage housing program for women and children who have been homeless; and Centro Familiar Guadalupano (Guadalupano Family Center) which offers several programs for young children (e.g., Head Start, Day Care) in conjunction with another social service agency and supports and encourages local artist groups.

The third and fourth program areas seem to reflect more recent community concerns as well as attempts to promote community empowerment through economic development and control. Thus, the third program area focuses on home ownership and financial services. Programs under this division seek both to educate families on property ownership issues and to facilitate investment by residents and financial institutions into the community (The Resurrection Project, 1998a). A key program in this area is the New Homes program which has developed low-income housing for Pilsen residents to replace some of the dilapidated, neglected, and abandoned structures and vacant lots in the community. Loan packaging assistance is currently available and TRP is in the process of expanding its financial services to offer its own savings and loan options to the community (The Resurrection Project, 1998a).

The fourth and final program concerns real estate development and asset management. TRP develops and renovates community-owned real estate in a way which makes it sustainable and affordable (The Resurrection Project, 1998a). TRP owns a number of rental properties and oversees the physical, financial and tenant management of these properties. The organization is currently managing $25 million in development projects (The Resurrection Project, 1998a). A critical program in this division is a Construction Cooperative which is a cooperative of small minority-owned construction companies who are involved in constructing and rehabbing TRP housing.

By assuming a management role, and developing new affordable housing, TRP has been able to increase the number of affordable housing units available to residents in the community and slow down displacement resulting from the recent increases in rent and housing costs associated with the proliferation of higher priced housing developments. Further, TRP is not an absentee landlord. Rather, its members have a critical stake in what happens to the community and its housing stock.

DISCUSSION AND CONCLUSIONS

Rubin and Rubin (1992) define community organizing as "bringing people together to combat shared problems and to increase their say about decisions that affect their lives" (p. 3). They argue that community organizing involves a search for social power and an effort to combat perceived helplessness through learning that what appears personal is often political (Rubin and Rubin, 1992, p. 1). Further, they maintain that organizing has the power not only to develop people's skills, their sense of efficacy, competence, and self-worth, but also to transform society, for it creates a capacity for democracy and for sustained social change (Rubin and Rubin, 1992, p. 3).

Borgos and Douglas (1996) note that essential elements of successful community organization include: (1) a participative culture in which participation in the organizing effort is seen as an end in itself and individuals are encouraged to do for themselves rather than letting others do for them; (2) a climate of inclusiveness; (3) breadth of mission and vision; and (4) a critical perspective (toward political, economic and social institutions) (p. 21). They define this last element as the most distinctive quality of direct-action community organizations and note that in many communities, community organizations are the only force promoting institutional accountability and responsiveness. A critical question is whether The Resurrection Project is engaged in these activities and whether the components necessary for successful organizing exist. Since this article is based on official documentation, and input from only a limited number of TRP's members, our conclusions are, at best, speculative. However, based on these sources, we can draw some tentative conclusions.

Officially, TRP's Mission Statement highlights a number of principles which reflect a participative and inclusive culture. The Principles of Operation require members to respect individual dignity and self-determination as well as the multiplicity of community interests represented by its membership, and to value cultural, religious and ethnic diversity (The Resurrection Project, 1989). The Principles also state that TRP strives to empower its members by promoting the idea that it need not do for others what they can do for themselves and by adhering to the belief that values find their deepest meaning when they are dignified by action (The Resurrection Project, 1989).

Community members are provided with a number of avenues by which to participate in TRP's efforts. They can take part in committees or they may be encouraged and supported by other community members who are part of TRP, to take on leadership roles in organizing efforts. Specific organizing activities rely upon the identification of local leaders using natural community networks and connections to locate those who may best represent the views of their neighbors. Of paramount importance are parish relationships. Indeed, such networks were critical to the organization's initial development and appear to continue to provide a strong ongoing base of support.

This raises the question, of course, as to whether the organization merely reflects the agenda of the community's churches, rather than its people. To some extent, this question is irrelevant in a community such as Pilsen where the church has historically played such a strong role in community issues and church participation is so broad. It is unlikely that the church's agenda differs vastly from the issues of the larger community. Further, efforts to include representatives from community organizations and businesses, as well as from institutions outside of the community in the organizational structure may provide a check, of sorts, on the likelihood that the organizational agenda is too heavily influenced by the concerns of its participant churches.

A more likely problem, however, raised by Father Dahm in his own analysis of lessons learned from past organizing activities in the community, is the possibility of creating a political elite among those church members who are active in community organizing efforts (Dahm and Harper, 1999). Father Dahm notes that to avoid such outcomes, churches must develop strategies for "conscientizing and involving the base, or grassroots" in organizing efforts (Dahm and Harper, 1999, p. 173). This philosophy is supported officially in TRP's mission statement and operating principles, which state that the organization promotes a democratic decision-making model and values the development and growth of people over the successful accomplishment of ends (The Resurrection Project, 1989). In addition, community organizing activities appear to be designed to broaden the participatory base of the organization, as do opportunities for taking part in the various program committees.

An important and related issue concerns whether the organizational agenda has depth, breadth and vision. Theories of community mobilization contend that organizers are likely to be most successful at motivating community members when they pick problems that are of immediate interest to them (Rubin and Rubin, 1992). Rubin and Rubin (1992) note that immediate problems, which are easily addressed are perhaps most useful since success in overcoming such problems may encourage people to move on to larger issues that require more resources and efforts. At the same time, organizations that maintain too specific a focus, which are unable to "bootstrap" from this initial success to broader issues, may fail to survive. Clearly, TRP's organizational foci are diverse, encompassing immediate concerns such as housing, long term issues such as economic development, and areas of cultural relevance like family life. Avenues for input related to program direction, through the organization's committee structure, in theory help to insure that people with close ethnic and personal connections to the community, who are keenly aware of community and ethnic norms, values, issues and concerns, remain deeply involved in setting the agenda.

The question of whether TRP maintains a critical perspective in relation to institutional accountability is more difficult to answer. The organization's efforts to develop alternative economic resources for community members can perhaps be read as a criticism of existing financial institutions. Yet TRP maintains ties with and seeks to engage such community financial institutions in its organizing efforts (Dahm and Harper, 1999). Indeed, to a large extent, TRP's activities seem to be focused on building community capacity, both in terms of promoting economic self-sufficiency and supporting existing social networks. Rather than directly confronting and challenging existing community structures, TRP seems to be emphasizing the development of alternatives. This emphasis may be related to cultural norms that do not encourage confrontation, especially in a community known to be a port of entry for first-generation immigrants, some of whom may be here illegally. Further, the importance of inclusiveness as an operating principle of TRP may play a role. Social action campaigns do not generally promote inclusion (Rothman, 1979). However, it is also possible that the absence of greater conflict is related to Pilsen's community identity. Pilsen appears to be a community in which its members not only share a common geographic border, but also ethnic and to a large extent economic solidarity. As such, there may be fewer factions within the community. Organizing efforts addressing community issues may be more inclusive than might be the case in more ethnically and economically diverse neighborhoods. While this is speculative, the fact that TRP members are more engaged in potentially confrontational activities at the metropolitan level lends some support to this explanation. For example, TRP is a member of United Power for Justice, a coalition of churches, institutions and not-for-profit organizations which specifically focuses on holding elected officials accountable and insuring that critical human services are available in under-served communities. Promoting resident involvement in this coalition is a strong emphasis of community organizing efforts.

Is TRP an example of a successful community organization, then? It is seemingly inclusive, promoting broad-based community participation and seeking to identify and address community problems as identified by community members themselves. It has a broad agenda which it seeks to carry out using strategies that emphasize consensus and unity. While all community members are not necessarily engaged in the organization's efforts, TRP ostensibly attempts to develop and nurture community leaders from all neighborhoods in its community organizing efforts. Further, through its Home Ownership and Financial Services activities, the organization is working to provide information and financial resources to community residents so that they can become property owners and prevent outside interests from taking over their community. TRP is apparently aware of the economic issues at stake and has taken an active role to become a "player." It serves as landlord and lender so that the community may maintain its identity and its unity. Further, the organization's character reflects and compliments the values of the community, with its strong roots in the community's parishes and its commitment to preserving the community's cultural identity. These characteristics and efforts suggest that TRP is indeed a successful and vibrant community organization, one which has been able to give residents a sense of power over their individual lives and the life of their community.

REFERENCES

Adelman, W. J. (1983). *Pilsen and the West Side* (2nd ed.). Chicago: Illinois Labor History Society, Ralph Helstein Fund for Education in Labor History.

Baker, A. D. (1995). The social production of space of two Chicago neighborhoods: Pilsen and Lincoln Park. Doctoral dissertation. University of Illinois at Chicago, Department of Sociology, Chicago, IL.

Borgos, S. & Douglas, S. (1996). Community organizing and community renewal: A view from the south. *Social Policy, 27*,18-29.

Brueggemann, W. G. (1996). *The practice of macro social work.* Chicago: Nelson-Hall.

Chicago Board of Education (1997). *1997 School report card, Juarez High School.* Chicago, IL: Author.

Conrad, K. M. & Cooksey, J. A. (1997). *Chicago's Pilsen–A community profile.* Chicago: University of Illinois at Chicago.

Dahm, C. W. & Harper, N. (1999). St Pius V Roman Catholic Church and the Pilsen area Resurrection Project. In N. Harper (Ed.), *Urban churches, vital signs: Beyond charity toward justice* (pp. 168-181). Grand Rapids, MI: Eerdmans.

Fellin, P. (1995). *The community and the social worker.* Itasca, IL: F. E. Peacock

Gartland, J. (1996, September) *Saint Procopius: Yesterday, today, and tomorrow's parish.* [Brochure]. Chicago, IL.

George, R. (1998, Fall). The business of education. *Company,* 2-5.

Illinois Criminal Justice Information Authority (1996, September). Street gangs and crime. *Research Bulletin.*

Kurson, B. (1996, November 8). A sense of place: The unabashed style of Chicago's Pilsen. *Chicago Sun Times.*

Lanier, A. S. (1988, October). Doing it their way: Why Pilsen is so . . . stubborn. *Chicago Enterprise,* 16-20.

Lauerman, C. (1995, September 12). Barrio is no barrier. *Chicago Tribune.*

Lutton, L. (1998, April 24). Will development bury the Barrio? *Chicago Reader, 27,* 1;16-30.

Montiel, M. & Ortego y Gasca, F. (1998). Chicanos, community, and change. In F. G. Rivera & J. L. Erlich (Eds.). *Community organizing in a diverse society* (pp. 43-61). Boston: Allyn and Bacon.

Pacyga, D. & Skerrett, E. (1986). *Chicago city of neighborhoods: Histories and tours.* Chicago: Loyola University Press.

Puente, T. (1998, February 11). Bills offer homeowner tax breaks. *Chicago Tribune* (Metro Chicago section). N8.

The Resurrection Project (1989). *Principles of operation.* [Unpublished manual]. Chicago, IL: Author.

The Resurrection Project (1998a) *Fact sheet.* [Unpublished manual]. Chicago, IL: Author.

The Resurrection Project (1998b). *Committee system fact sheet.* [Unpublished manual]. Chicago, IL: Author.

Ritter, J. (1997, April 21). Pilsen fears UIC expansion. *Chicago Sun Times.* (Metro Chicago section).

Rivera, F. & Erlich, J. (1998). *Community organizing in a diverse society.* Boston: Allyn and Bacon.

Rothman, J. (1979). Three models of community organization practice, their mixing and phasing. In F. M. Cox, J. L. Erlich, J. Rothman & J. E. Tropman (Eds.), *Strategies of community organization* (pp. 25-45). Itasca, IL: F. E. Peacock.

Rubin, H. J. & Rubin, I. S. (1992). *Community organizing and development.* Boston: Allyn and Bacon.

Schultz, S. (1998, April 30). TIF battle boils down to politics. *Chicago Sun Times.*

Spergel, I. A. & Grossman, S. F. (1996). P*reliminary evaluation of the Little Village Gang Violence Reduction Project: A case study of a "successful" program.* [Unpublished report]. Chicago, IL: School of Social Service Administration.

University of Illinois, Nathalie P. Voorhees Center for Neighborhood and Community Improvement and Chicago Rehab Network (1995a). *Development without displacement task force background paper* [Online]. Available: Http://www.uic.edu/~pwright/dwd.html#pilsen.

University of Illinois, Nathalie P. Voorhees Center for Neighborhood and Community Improvement in partnership with The Resurrection Project (1995b, December). *Pilsen rent study.* [Unpublished report]. Chicago, IL: Author.

The 1996 Chicago Latino Registered Voter Political Survey: Political Participation and Public Policy Positions

David K. Jesuit
Angela Nirchi
Maria Vidal de Haymes
Peter M. Sanchez

SUMMARY. The Latino population in the United States has been expanding at a tremendous rate in recent decades and as the number of Latinos in the United States grows, so does their potential for influencing American politics grow. Yet, we have a very limited understanding of Latino civic engagement, political behavior, and public policy opinions. This article presents the results of a survey of 408 registered Latino voters in Chicago, Illinois. The findings advance a multidimensional understanding of Latino political behaviors and attitudes through the examination of multiple measures of political participation and opinions concerning political parties and public issues such as welfare reform, immigration, naturalization and official language policy, bilingual education, capital punishment, gun control, and affirmative action.

David K. Jesuit is affiliated with the Loyola University Political Science Department.

Angela Nirchi, MSW, is affiliated with the University of Chicago Children's Hospital.

Maria Vidal de Haymes, PhD, is affiliated with the Loyola University School of Social Work.

Peter M. Sanchez, PhD, is affiliated with the Loyola University Political Science Department.

[Haworth co-indexing entry note]: "The 1996 Chicago Latino Registered Voter Political Survey: Political Participation and Public Policy Positions." Jesuit, David K. et al. Co-published simultaneously in *Journal of Poverty* (The Haworth Press, Inc.) Vol. 4, No. 1/2, 2000, pp. 151-165; and: *Latino Poverty in the New Century: Inequalities, Challenges and Barriers* (ed: Maria Vidal de Haymes, Keith M. Kilty, and Elizabeth A. Segal) The Haworth Press, Inc., 2000, pp. 151-165. Single or multiple copies of this article are available for a fee from The Haworth Document Delivery Service [1-800-342-9678, 9:00 a.m. - 5:00 p.m. (EST). E-mail address: getinfo@haworthpressinc.com].

Findings are discussed in the context of earlier studies of Latino electoral participation and American public policy opinions. *[Article copies available for a fee from The Haworth Document Delivery Service: 1-800-342-9678. E-mail address: <getinfo@haworthpressinc.com> Website: <http://www. haworthpressinc.com>]*

KEYWORDS. Latino voters, public policy opinions, electoral participation, political parties

INTRODUCTION

The Latino population in the United States has been expanding at a tremendous rate over the last two decades, so much so that it is predicted that Latinos will become the largest ethnic minority group shortly after the turn of the century. In 1990, one out of every ten persons counted in the U.S. census was Latino, and the Bureau of the Census projects that by the year 2050 one of every five U.S. residents may be Latino (U.S. Bureau of the Census 1993:2). As the number of Latinos in the United States grows, so does their potential for influencing American politics grow. Yet, we have a very limited understanding of Latino civic engagement, political behavior, and public policy opinions.

Despite the fact that political surveys are conducted and released on a daily basis during campaign seasons, the vast majority fail to offer useful information to political activists in at least two ways. For one, most political surveys are designed to determine only the candidate preferences of the respondents and perhaps ask for their opinions concerning a few of the most high profile issues on the campaign. Secondly, the overwhelming majority of these polls are designed to make statistical inferences to the population as a whole and therefore they sample a representative cross-section, which does not include a sufficient number of Latinos, or other minorities within the population to allow for any statistical inferences to be drawn concerning their attitudes and behavior. Arvizu and Garcia have pointed out that "[T]he omission of ethnicity by most major voting studies and data sets has created an incomplete and inaccurate depiction of the American voting public" (1996: 110).

Political surveys have historically ignored, undercounted, or oversimplified Latino political behavior. It has been in only the last two decades that researchers have begun to give serious attention to Latino political participation. Most of the research thus far, however, is limited to comparisons of Latino with Anglo voting rates.

LITERATURE REVIEW

Perhaps the first attempt to understand Latino voting behavior can be found in Wolfinger and Rosenstone's, *Who Votes* (1980). Their findings indicated that while Chicanos were three percent more likely to vote than the general population, when controlling for socioeconomic status, their potential political power was compromised by high levels of noncitizenship and low naturalization rates. Similarly, Calvo and Rosenstone (1989) noted the diluted voter potential among Latinos due to lack of citizenship. Interestingly, Garcia and Arce (1988) found higher voter turnout rates among naturalized and first generation, American-born Chicanos in contrast to second generation and beyond Chicano citizens.

Nearly a decade later, Calvo and Rosenstone (1989) reported Latino voter turnout to be 51.8%, 15 percentage points lower than that of the U.S. in general, contradicting Wolfinger and Rosenstone's earlier findings. However, Calvo and Rosenstone found considerable ethnic group differences among Latinos, with Cuban turnout rates exceeding that of non-Latino voters and Puerto Ricans to be the least likely to vote among Latinos. Similarly, de la Garza and others (1992) found Latino participation to lag substantially behind that of non-Latinos.

More recently, Diaz (1996) indicated that Latino voter registration rates were approximately 20% lower than those of non-Latinos, in the 1990, 1992, and 1994 election years. Diaz also found ethnic variation in voter registration rates when analyzing data from the Latino National Political Survey. For example, he found that approximately 66% of Mexican Americans, 65% of Puerto Ricans, and 83% of Cuban Americans were registered to vote. Furthermore, he found that approximately 78% of Mexican Americans, 74% of Puerto Ricans, and 88% of Cuban Americans had ever registered to vote.

Previous studies of the general electorate have indicated that participation in electoral politics is positively associated with increases in socioeconomic status (Verba & Nie 1972). There is some evidence of a similar pattern among Latinos. Higher levels of educational attainment and occupational status were found to increase Mexican and

Puerto Rican voter turnout, while having virtually no effect on Cuban voting (Calvo & Rosenstone 1989). Calvo and Rosenstone (1989) argue that, while education was found to be the best socioeconomic predictor of increased voting for the general U.S. population, its impact on Latinos, while significant was less pronounced. Wrinkle and others (1996) observed that increases in income promoted non-electoral political activity among Puerto Ricans, Mexican Americans, and Cubans, but found that increases in education had a positive effect on Puerto Rican and Mexican Americans only. Arvizu (1994, 1996) found the interaction between education and age to be important in predicting Latino voter turnout. Older, rather than younger, Mexican Americans and Puerto Ricans were found to be more likely to vote.

Gender has also been identified in previous research as a significant factor in Latino political participation and opinion formation. Welch and Sigelman (1992) uncovered a gender gap among Latinos on measures of political ideology, party identification, and presidential voting. Wrinkle and others (1996) also identified gender as a significant predictor of nonelectoral political activity among Mexican Americans. They found Chicanas were more likely to write letters, attend public meetings, and engage in other nonelectoral political activities than their male counterparts.

Hero and Campbell (1996) found that, while Latinos may be less likely to vote than non-Latinos, Latino participation in a number of other nonelectoral political forums was not distinct when socioeconomic differences were considered. More specifically, when socioeconomic variation is accounted for, there is not a significant difference between Latino and non-Latino nonvoting political participation, such as attending public meetings, writing to public officials, attending rallies, and contributing money. Significant differences between the two groups were found only in the rates of volunteering for a candidate or party and signing petitions.

Wrinkle and others (1996) found that participation in nonelectoral political activities increases for all Latino groups with higher incomes, similar to patterns observed in voting behavior in the general population. They also found that nonelectoral political participation was boosted by increased levels of education among Puerto Ricans and Mexican Americans. And, they found age to be significant in predicting Mexican American and Puerto Rican nonelectoral political participation.

In summary, we can see that numerous factors have been found to affect Latino political participation. Both education and income seem to be positively related to political participation, with education clearly the stronger predictor. Numerous studies have also found age to influence political activity, with older individuals participating at higher levels than younger individuals. Finally, there have been varied findings concerning the effects of gender and ethnicity on voter participation. Some studies have indicated that while women voted with less frequency than men prior to the 1970s, the gap has been closed in recent decades. Other research has shown that Latinas participate at higher rates than Latino men in nonelectoral political activities.

While voting is an important measure of political participation, it does not capture other forms of civic engagement, such as participation in political organizations or other private voluntary associations (e.g., charities, community groups, religious organizations). A multidimensional conceptualization of political participation incorporates a broad spectrum of citizen mobilization like voting, campaigning, participation in community activities, involvement in collective action to solve a problem, public discourse, and many other forms of nonelectoral political activity. Furthermore, some analysts have argued elsewhere that taking part in private voluntary associations is strongly associated with voting and other political activity (Verba & Nie 1972, Putnam 1994, Diaz 1996). Thus a view that incorporates both electoral and nonelectoral political behaviors provides a more accurate picture of civic engagement and political participation.

In this study, we attempt to gain a multidimensional understanding of Latino political behaviors and attitudes by examining multiple measures of political participation and opinions concerning political parties and public issues.

METHODOLOGY AND SAMPLE DESCRIPTION

Methodology

In order to collect data on Latino political participation and public policy preferences, we developed a 54-question telephone survey, which was administered during a two-week period in late-October 1996, just prior to the national elections. We collected data on demographic characteristics, nonelectoral and electoral political participation, public policy opinions, and candidate choices. The instrument contained both multiple choice and open-ended questions. The questionnaire was piloted on a small number of individuals and modified according to the feedback received. The survey instrument was administered principally by nearly 40 volunteers in both Spanish and English, and required approximately 20 minutes to complete.

Sample

The Cook County Board of Elections provided two electronic files for the purpose of drawing a sample. One file contained a complete list of all registered voters in Chicago, with phone numbers when available. The second file contained a list of Latino surnames developed by the U.S. Census Bureau. The total list of registered voters (N = 1,374,644) was matched with the Latino surname file, yielding 141,659 estimated Latino registered voters for the city of Chicago. While only a sample size of 400 was needed to achieve a 5% confidence interval, a 5% random sample of voters with phone numbers was drawn from this file to generate a list for conducting the survey. This larger sample was drawn to insure that a sufficient number of cases would be available for the study in the event of: (1) our inability to locate persons appearing on the list due to wrong numbers, disconnected phones, not at home when called, or move in residence, (2) persons appearing on the list who did not meet study criterion (e.g., persons with Spanish surnames who were not Latino), and (3) individuals declining participation in the study. This master list was run in random order to produce sub-lists for individual volunteers conducting the phone interviews. A total of 408 surveys were completed during the two-week period, yielding a sample size sufficient for a 5% confidence interval.

The sample represented the following general characteristics. Women comprised 61 percent of all respondents. With regard to national origin, 46.7% were of Mexican heritage, 37.7% were Puerto Rican, and 15.6% were of other Latino heritage. Sample frequencies and means indicated that the typical Latino registered voter was 40 years old, had some college education (30.9%), was foreign born (54.2%), had immigrated to the U.S. at 18 years of age, was married (54.3%), and was overwhelmingly of the Catholic faith (77.1%). Furthermore, the average Latino registered voter lived in a four-member household

(3.74), in which Spanish is more likely to be spoken (43%), and was a full-time employee (52.5%), with a total annual family income of $20,000 to $29,000.

FINDINGS AND DISCUSSION

Political Participation

In this study, political participation was measured broadly, consisting of electoral and non-electoral political mobilization. Participants were asked about their voting behavior, involvement in political organizations, and community or religious organizations. In our analysis of the political participation data, which is detailed elsewhere (Sanchez & Vidal de Haymes 1997), we constructed a simple four-point index of political participation based on a combination of variables that measured voting, activity in political organizations, and activity in community organizations, to identify predictors of political participation.

Our results indicated that voting was best explained by two variables: how long the respondent had been registered to vote and the age of the respondent. Voting was found to increase with age and length of time registered to vote. We found that male gender, level of education, and the length of time the respondent had resided in the U.S. were positively related, and the strongest determinants of whether an individual will participate in a political organization. Education was the only factor that significantly predicted whether a respondent was involved in a community or religious organization.

Our data tend to corroborate the findings of previous studies in a limited manner. As in other studies, our data support the notion that education is positively related to political participation. Those Latinos with higher levels of education tend to be more active politically than those with lower education levels. Additionally, we found that maturity, or simply time, has a positive effect on participation. Those who are older or have been in the United States longer tend to participate more than those who are younger or have been in the United States only for a short time.

Our study, on the other hand, yielded some new and interesting findings. For example, our data suggest that women tend to participate at lower levels than men. We could not reach any conclusions about why women seem to be less active politically than men without collecting and analyzing more data. Our findings were surprising because our sample was composed of 60% women. Since there are more men than women in the Chicago Latino population, we were convinced that Latinas were much more likely to register to vote than Latino men since our random sample of registered voters yielded a 6 to 4 ratio of female to male registered voters, and consequently we expected to find that women would be more active politically.

Our study uncovered a predictor of political participation–how long a respondent has been registered to vote–that has not been explored in the past. Those Latinos who have been registered to vote for more than four years tend to participate at higher rates than those who have recently registered. This finding suggests that in a period of large-scale Latino voter registration, such as the Latino Vote 96 campaign that was underway during the time of the study, the Latino vote may not be immediately perceptible. However, in the long run, registration efforts will yield large dividends.

What we did not find is also very interesting. For example, it appears that Latinos who were born in the United States are no more likely to participate politically than Latinos who are immigrants. Likewise, Latinos who speak Spanish predominantly in their homes are not less likely to participate politically than those who speak English principally. Being more "American," as defined by speaking English or being born in the United States, does not seem to increase political participation, at least among those who are citizens and registered to vote.

Another important observation is that we did not find a very strong relationship between education and age and political participation. This could be due to the fact that Latinos may be motivated to participate politically by other factors than the population at large, or more specifically than the Anglo population. One of the questions in our survey asked the respondents whether they thought their political participation would increase if there were more Latinos running for public office. The results were quite startling: 61% said that their participation would increase or dramatically increase. Latino political participation, like the participation of other minorities, may be greatly affected by the fact that candidates do not usually come from their ethnic group. If Latinos knew that they were going to be represented by a Latino it is much more likely that their political participation would follow the general patterns of Anglo voters. Thus, when Latinos can vote for Latinos to represent them we may see increased levels of participation, and participation patterns that resemble more closely the patterns of Anglo voters.

Party Affiliation and Public Policy Opinions

Party Affiliation. The party preferences of Latino voters in Chicago were decidedly Democratic in 1996, with 79.9% identifying themselves as either a Democrat or Strong Democrat. This is somewhat puzzling when one considers the fact that only 29.5% of the respondents say that they consider themselves to be to the left of center ideologically (socialist 5.1%, very liberal 4.5%, and liberal 19.9%), yet it is possible that this apparent paradox is due to cultural preferences for being conservative socially as well as the perception that the Democratic Party has moved to the center of the ideological spectrum. Furthermore, 72.3% of Latinos stated their intent to vote for President Clinton in the 1996 election, 4.3% for Dole, and 20% were either undecided or unfamiliar with the candidates.

Welfare Reform. There was a series of six questions that addressed the welfare reforms that had been recently debated in Congress. Our results indicated that a significant number of Latinos in Chicago favor some reforms in the welfare system. For example, 49.8% felt that welfare benefits should be cut off after a period of two years and 81.1% thought that people should receive welfare only if they perform some sort of work for those benefits. These findings suggest a reasonably strong reform sentiment among Latinos. However, when asked if parents on welfare should receive some sort of government funded day care in order to work or study, 88% of the respondents agreed, and 90.5% thought that legal residents of the U.S. should be eligible for welfare benefits, education, and health care. In addition, an overwhelming 92.1% of registered Latinos in Chicago believe that the government should establish a national health care system. In sum, Latinos in Chicago favor some of the major welfare reforms recently adopted by Congress and the President, particularly the work requirements. However, there is overall support for the social welfare state and a rejection of many of the more stringent provisions included in the compromise welfare reform package (see Table 1).

These views on welfare reform are similar to those found in a 1993 national study of public opinions of the general registered voter population (Garin, Molyneux, & DiVall 1994:47). The study concluded that while voters accepted a conservative diagnosis of the problem, they did not accept a conservative agenda for reform. More specifically, they found that 93% of voters were in favor of requiring welfare recipients to work for their welfare checks and 65% favored a general two-year limit on benefits. Yet, 95% supported the provision of child

TABLE 1. Chicago Latino Registered Voter Public Policy (Opinion)

Issue	Agree		Neutral		Disagree	
	f	%	f	%	f	%
Welfare benefits should be cut after a period of 2 years.	201	49.8	40	9.9	162	40.2
People should perform work for welfare benefits, unless they have a disability.	331	81.1	22	5.4	55	13.5
Parents on welfare should receive subsidized day care, to allow them to work or study.	358	88.0	19	4.7	30	7.3
Children of legal residents should be eligible for welfare, education, and health care benefits.	368	90.5	17	4.2	22	5.4
The government should establish a national health care system that covers all citizens.	375	92.1	20	4.9	12	2.9
The minimum wage should be increased.	372	91.4	17	4.2	18	4.4
The government should take stronger steps to limit immigration to the U.S.	204	50.5	84	20.8	116	28.7
It should be easier to become a citizen of the U.S.	237	58.5	78	19.3	90	22.2
It should be easier to become a registered voter.	283	69.9	62	15.3	60	14.8
English should be the official language of the U.S.	136	33.4	31	7.6	240	59.0
The government should increase spending for bilingual education.	320	79.0	36	8.9	49	12.1
The government should eliminate affirmative action.	128	31.8	58	14.4	217	53.9
The federal government should strengthen gun control.	353	86.7	16	3.9	38	9.4
The death penalty should be used in the criminal justice system.	232	58.6	57	14.4	107	27.0
Money has too much influence in American politics and elections.	381	93.8	12	3.0	13	3.2
The government should reimburse parents if they choose to send their children to private school.	219	54.3	55	13.6	129	32.1

care subsidies and 89% supported the provision of health care benefits to parents on welfare who go to work.

Immigration and Citizenship. In addition to welfare issues, we included several questions that are of special interest to Latinos, such as immigration and citizenship. Half (50.5%) believe that the U.S. government should take stronger steps to limit immigration into the U.S., while 58.5% agree that it should be easier to become a U.S. citizen (see Table 1). These results are somewhat contradictory and suggest that despite the fact that the survey item did not specify "legal or illegal" immigration, many respondents were probably thinking in those terms. Nonetheless, it is evident that Latinos who have established citizenship in the U.S. support some restrictions on additional immigration and are much more likely to support the maintenance of benefits to current immigrants rather than efforts to ease entry into the United States. Perhaps this position can be attributed to the issue that Latinos are more likely than Anglos to be adversely affected by the economic impact of additional immigration (Miller, Polinard, & Wrinkle 1985). Whatever the reason, the current wave of restrictionist attitudes among immigrants has a long history in the U.S. Epenshade and Hempstead (1996) indicate that this "drawbridge" mentality has existed in this nation since the time of the pilgrims.

While half of the Latino respondents in our survey supported some steps to limit immigration, a CBS News/*New York Times* general public opinion poll conducted in June of 1993 indicated that nearly two-thirds of survey respondents thought the level of U.S. immigration should be lowered, roughly one-third felt that immigrants take jobs away from native workers, and half felt that immigrants cause problems for the U.S. (Espenshade & Hempstead 1996:44-45). A national poll conducted by the *Wall Street Journal* and NBC News in 1996, revealed that 52% of respondents wanted to halt all immigration, illegal or legal, for five years (Reimers 1998:30)

English Only. Another area of particular interest to Latinos concerns efforts to make English the official language. These movements have garnered some momentum in states with large Latino populations within the last few years and the Republican Party has attempted to use this issue as a potential "wedge." In fact, studies of public opinion in this area have indicated that majorities (64.5%) of the general public support these efforts (Tatalovich 1995:179). We found that 59% of Chicago Latinos oppose the adoption of English as the official language, which is consistent with previous research (e.g., de la Garza, Falcon, Garcia, & Garcia 1992). We also found strong support (79%) for increased government funding for bilingual education (see Table 1). In short, efforts to make English the official language will continue to be a divisive issue within the electorate, with Latinos being the main opposition group to the English-only movement.

Affirmative Action. As evidenced by the mobilization of Latinos and other groups in California, the elimination of affirmative action programs is an issue which has the potential to activate grassroots movements and inspire individual citizens to participate. Our results indicate that 53.9% of Latinos in Chicago favor affirmative action programs (see Table 1). These figures place Latino support for affirmative action between that of White and Black Americans. Kinder and Sanders (1996:17) indicate that 15.4% of Whites and 67.7% of African Americans support affirmative action programs in the work place and 29.7% and 79.7%, respectively, support such programs in college admissions.

Capital Punishment and Gun Control. A review of public opinion and capital punishment research indicates that approximately 75% of the American public support the death penalty when they are not presented with the alternative of a life sentence without parole (McGarrell & Sandys 1996:501). A recent Gallup poll found that 7 out of 10 Americans support the death penalty for individuals convicted of murder, even though many of those same people believe American minorities and the poor are most likely to receive a death sentence. While our study did not find such overwhelming support for capital punishment, we did find considerable support among Latinos (58.6%). (See Table 1.)

There was overwhelming support among the survey respondents for strengthening gun control laws. Eighty-seven percent of respondents favored increased federal government restrictions on gun ownership (see Table 1). This strong support for more stringent gun control laws is also shared by the general American public. A June 1999 Gallup poll found that 89% of Americans surveyed supported mandatory prison sentences for felons who commit crimes with guns; 87% supported mandatory background checks for gun purchasers; 82% agreed with raising the minimum age for handgun possession to 21 years of age; and 79% supported mandatory registration of all firearms (Gallup 1999).

Government Spending. Study participants were asked to identify which of four areas of government spending should be cut the most if needed to balance the national budget: corporate subsidies and tax breaks, education, defense, and social welfare programs. More than half (53%) of respondents indicated that corporate subsidies and tax breaks should be cut and nearly a third (29.3%) supported defense cuts. There was considerably less support for cuts in social welfare program (14.3%) and education (2.9%) spending.

Major Problems in the U.S. Facing Latinos. Respondents were also asked to reflect on what they believed to be the most important contemporary problems facing Latinos in the U.S. This survey item was open-ended. The most frequent responses in rank order were: discrimination/racism (26.8%), the economy and employment prospects (15.7%), crime/gangs/and drugs (15.2%), education (13.9%), immigration (9%), lack of political representation (6.2%), welfare (6.2%), anti-immigrant/Latino legislation (3.6%).

CONCLUSION

The results of our analysis indicate that the length of time an immigrant has lived in the U.S., age, education, and how long the respondent has been registered to vote, are all positively related to levels of political participation. Latinas tend to participate at lower levels than their male counterparts. Young citizens have the lowest rates of registration and voting and our results indicate that the length of time one has been registered is an important determinant of other forms of political participation. Lastly, a majority of respondents indicated that their levels of political participation would increase if more Latino candidates ran for public office.

Although it is evident that more research on the political attitudes and party affiliation of Latinos in Chicago needs to be conducted, our study was able to identify several important characteristics of Latino public opinion. For example, identification with the Democratic Party by Latinos in Chicago is extremely high. This level of support might be explained by the Democratic positions on such issues as moderate welfare reform, increases in the minimum-wage, and health care reform, which Latinos strongly favor. Although the issues of English only, immigration, and affirmative action do not enjoy the widespread support that one might think among registered Latino voters in Chicago, our results indicate that slim to moderate majorities reject English-only legislation and support affirmative action and restrictions on immigration. Furthermore, Latinos would rather see cuts in federal spending for corporate tax incentives and defense, than cuts in educational and social welfare programming to balance the budget.

BIBLIOGRAPHY

Andersen, K. (1975). Working women and political participation, 1952-1972. *American Journal of Political Science, 19*, 439-453.

Arvizu, J. R. (1994). *National origin based variations of Latino voter turnout in 1988: Findings from the Latino national political survey*, working paper, 21 Tucson, AZ: Mexican American Studies and Research Center, University of Arizona.

Arvizu, J. R. and Garcia, F. C. (1996). Latino voting participation: Explaining and differentiating Latino voting turnout. *Hispanic Journal of Behavioral Sciences, 18*(2), 104-128.

Calvo, M. A. and Rosenstone, S. J. (1989). *Hispanic political participation* (Latino Electorates Series). San Antonio, TX: Southwest Voter Research Institute.

Conway, M. M. (1985). *Political participation in the United States*. Washington, DC: Congressional Quarterly Press.

de la Garza, R. O., Falcon, A., Garcia, F. C., and Garcia, J. A., and (1992). Hispanic Americans in the Mainstream of U.S. Politics. *The Public Perspective 3*(5), 19-23.

de la Garza, R. O., DeSipio, L., Garcia, F. C., Garcia, J., and Falcon, A. (1992). *Latino voices: Mexican, Puerto Rican, and Cuban perspectives on American politics*. Boulder, CO: Westview.

Diaz, W. (1996). Latino participation in America: Associational and political roles. *Hispanic Journal of Behavioral Sciences*, 18(2), 154-174.

Espenshade, T. J. and Hempstead, K. (1996). Contemporary American Attitudes Towards U.S. Immigration. *International Migration Review*, 30(2), 535-570.

Gallup News Service (June 16, 1999). Americans Support Wide Variety of Gun Control Measures. www.gallup.com/poll/release/pr990616.asp.

Gallup News Service (February 24, 1999). Public Opinion Supports the Death Penalty. www.gallup.com/poll/release/pr990224.asp.

Garcia, J. A., and Arce, C. H. (1988). Political orientations and behaviors of Chicanos: Trying to make sense out of attitudes and participation. In F. C. Garcia (Ed.), *Latinos and the political system*. Notre Dame, IN: University of Notre Dame Press.

Garin, G., Molyneux, G., and DiVall, L. (1994). Public Attitudes Toward Welfare Reform. *Social Policy, 25*, 44-49.

Gero, R. E. and Campbell, A. E. (1996). Understanding Latino political participation: Exploring evidence from the Latino national political survey. *Hispanic Journal of Behavioral Sciences, 18*(2), 129-141.

Kinder, D. R., and Sanders, L. M. (1996). *Divided by Color: Racial Politics and Democratic Ideals*. Chicago, IL: The University of Chicago Press.

Miller, L. W., Polinard, J. L., and Wrinkle, R. D. (1985). Attitudes Toward Undocumented Workers: The Mexican American Perspective. In R. O. de la Garza, F. D. Bean, C. M. Bonjean, R. Romo, and R. Alvarez (Eds.) *The Mexican American Experience: An Interdisciplinary Anthology.*

McGarrell, E. F. and Sandys, M. (1996). The Misperception of Public Opinion Toward Capital Punishment. *American Behavioral Scientist, 39*(4), 500-513.

Putnam, R. D. (1994). *Making democracy work: Civic traditions in modern Italy.* Princeton, NJ: Princeton University Press.

Reimers, D. M. (1998). *Unwelcome Strangers: American Identity and the Turn Against Immigration.* New York: Columbia University Press.

Romer, N. (1990). Is political activism still a masculine endeavor? *Psychology of Women Quarterly,* 14, 229-243.

Sanchez, Peter and Maria Vidal de Haymes. (1997). "Latino Electoral and Nonelectoral Political Participation: Findings from the 1996 Chicago Latino Registered Voter Survey." *Harvard Journal of Latino Public Policy,* 10:27-40.

Stanley, H. W., and Neimi, R. (1992). *Vital statistics on American politics.* Washington, DC: Congressional Quarterly Press.

Tatalovich, R. (1995). *Nativism Reborn: The Official English Language Movement and the American States.* Lexington, Kentucky: The University Press of Kentucky.

U.S. Bureau of the Census. (1993). *Hispanic Americans Today.* Washington, DC: U.S. Government Printing Office.

Verba, S., and Nie, N. H. (1972). *Participation in America: Political democracy and social equality.* New York: Harper and Row.

Verba S., Schlozman, K. L. and Brady, H. (1995). *Voice and equality: Civic volunteerism in American politics.* Cambridge, MA: Harvard University Press.

Welch, S. (1977). Women as political animals: A test of some explanations for male-female political participation differences. *American Journal of Political Science, 21,* 711-730.

Welch, S., and Sigleman, L. (1992). A gender gap among Hispanics? A comparison with Blacks and Anglos. *Western Political Quarterly, 45,* 181-199.

Wolfinger, R. E. and Rosenstone, S. E. (1980). *Who votes?* New Haven, CT: University Press Yale.

Wrinkle, R. D., Stewart, J. S., Polinard, J. L., Meier, K. J., and Arvizu, J. R. (1996). Ethnicity and nonelectoral political participation. *Hispanic Journal of Behavioral Sciences, 18*(2), 142-153.

THOUGHTS ON POVERTY
AND INEQUALITY

Citizenship 101:
Equality as an American Process

Elizabeth S. Mahler
Petra Alvarez
Santiago Angel
Miguel Delgado
Marta Perez
Erasmo Toledo
Bertha Tomas

Elizabeth S. Mahler has a Bachelor's in social work from Loyola University, Chicago. She volunteers in the citizenship program at Centro Romero, a Latino social service agency in Chicago's Edgewater neighborhood.

Petra Alvarez, Santiago Angel, Miguel Delgado, Marta Perez, Erasmo Toledo, and Bertha Tomas are all students in the citizenship program.

Translation provided by Kerry Doyle, co-volunteer in the citizenship class.

[Haworth co-indexing entry note]: "Citizenship 101: Equality as an American Process." Mahler, Elizabeth S. et al. Co-published simultaneously in *Journal of Poverty* (The Haworth Press, Inc.) Vol. 4, No. 1/2, 2000, pp. 167-171; and: *Latino Poverty in the New Century: Inequalities, Challenges and Barriers* (ed: Maria Vidal de Haymes, Keith M. Kilty, and Elizabeth A. Segal) The Haworth Press, Inc., 2000, pp. 167-171. Single or multiple copies of this article are available for a fee from The Haworth Document Delivery Service [1-800-342-9678, 9:00 a.m. - 5:00 p.m. (EST). E-mail address: getinfo@haworthpressinc.com].

I can't even begin to compare my situation with that of the people in my citizenship class. Compared to other kids and families around me in middle class America I had it tough: my parents were divorced, and my mom had to work nights for more money in order to support my two brothers and me. We were lucky to have the opportunities we did because it came from the extended support of my mom's parents and friends. In comparison to the rest of the world, I had abundant opportunities and privileges not afforded everyone. In addition, I was raised in and expected to know American society and how to get what I wanted out of it, and it was easily reciprocated to me.

"Teaching" citizenship started as a way to be involved in my community and do something new amidst the daily grind of social work practice. I have worked for the past three years predominantly with immigrants, but around different issues such as housing or case management. Instead, it has turned into a new history lesson for me–a reevaluation of how American culture and government incorporates its increasingly global community, and how it encourages the recognition of naturalized citizens as "Americans."

Question #61 (of the U.S. citizenship test): What is the *basic belief* of the United States of America as described by the Declaration of Independence? "THAT ALL MEN [sic] ARE CREATED EQUAL," says the Tuesday night citizenship class at Centro Romero, a Latino social-service agency on the north side of Chicago. This answer is easily recalled by the students, either out of hope or firm belief that it applies to them too, even though they are not yet citizens. According to American rhetoric, all people, citizens or not, are considered equal under the law. Yet the spirit of this premise as well as the legally binding nature of this belief is violated everyday, as experienced by this microcosm of Latino society in America.

After class was over, most of us stayed around to discuss our experiences and perceptions of inequality as it pertains to life in America. It is ironic upon reflection that right after discussing the basic belief of the United States that "all [people] are created equal," we moved into a discussion about inequality. Individuals and families immigrate to this country on the premise that there is equality, and we make them memorize that for their exams to obtain citizenship. As an Anglo and their "teacher," I was nervous at the reaction of the group. Would they think I was being too forward? Would they be honest with me? Or would they guard their answers so as not to hurt my feelings or not to disrespect a place that they are supposed to embrace? I think the result was a combination of mixed feelings and obvious conflict surrounding thoughts and feelings of inequality, yet desiring to highlight the positives of living in America. (Note: The students felt more comfortable speaking and describing their experiences in Spanish, and Kerry Doyle, the other co-teacher, was able to translate.)

Evidence shows in society and in our personal lives that the basic belief that "all men are created equal" is easier said than done. Through the testimonies of Petra, Erasmo, and Miguel you can hear the frustration and reflection of their own personal battle for equity and recognition that often is pushed aside for language, racial, and economic barriers. Even mastering the language is not enough to ensure equality, for the evidence of English as a Second Language is heard through the accent. "Even if you speak English, they notice an accent–a difference," reports Miguel. "They get mad if you don't speak correctly. They want you to speak exactly the way they do." Petra defined her language experience at work: "When you speak English you are treated better, especially on the job. The boss speaks to the English speakers more." The presence and perception of a language barrier alleges inequalities, according to this group. The issue of language is overarching and dictates the consideration of immigrants by the dominant society, showing itself specifically at the workplace and at the hospital. They see language as an accessory or a barrier to opportunities and services.

Erasmo's experiences take the workplace environment to another level of language-barrier separation. "There is a difference in treatment of U.S.-born and foreign-born. The harder work always goes to the foreign-born," he says with passion in his voice, evidence that he has decided not to be desensitized to such treatment. He is also one of the younger participants in the class, and this may be why such inequalities appear to be interpreted differently than others who shrug their shoulders when you say "that's not fair." Not only do foreign-born workers get tougher assignments, i.e., manual labor, "U.S.-born will get better jobs, even if they have the same skills as we do." Often the general population of America is ignorant of the fact that, although many immigrants cannot articulate themselves fluently in English, it does not mean they have less capabilities or aptitude. Instead we measure intelligence based on our own standard of comprehension, thereby underestimating others.

For some, reported experiences were positive and supportive. Santiago, a Mexican immigrant, had a positive experience with hospital care. He asserts that in his perspective he has a personal responsibility to advocate on his own behalf to access services, especially with paying expenses. He had been to the health clinic and could not pay all his bills. When he went for services he found the workers very helpful, and acquired fee adjustments according to his income. This group of students agreed that you must know the process and system of acquiring entitled services; if you do not have those tools, there are not many places that have the patience to see you through the process. Kerry Doyle, co-teacher of the class, volunteered on the Texas/Mexico border and said that most of her advocacy work took place in the hospitals or around health issues. She witnessed that much of the Spanish-speaking population would go untreated for longer periods of time due to the lack of understanding and language barriers between hospital staff and patients.

A deeper issue that seemed to surface was tension between being grateful and feeling resentment at the same time. The immigrant mentality is usually defined as people coming to America in search of greater opportunities and, more specifically, wealth. This mantra rings true with these adults. Marta came to the United States from Guatemala because she could not adequately provide for her children under the conditions of her home. She hopes that by living here and becoming a citizen she will make a path for her children to have a better life. Currently she is a housekeeper for a family in Chicago. Bertha, another older female student who recently passed her citizenship test, was eager to explain that she has never felt mistreated or unequally treated since coming to the United States. When she immigrated she connected with a church, which gave her food, found her and her children a place to stay, and she had a job within a few weeks. For this she is very grateful.

These experiences made me think about the American conceptualization of poverty and inequality. While equality is justice, it can be understood as relative to others' experiences, just as with the notion of poverty. Is it good enough to be treated unequally, but better than a previous experience? Is it good enough to be satisfied with doing better than you ever have before but still be living in poverty? Undoubtedly the answer is no, and most of us would want to believe it.

Using the notion of relative equality is not an excuse to take advantage of a person's apparent acceptance of her/his position in life. A female student, who has passed her citizenship exam, but still comes to class to practice English, and who works in a factory says she does not have time to study because she is allowed only a half hour break for lunch. Unfortunately, it seems as if people in power, such as employers and other professionals, can manipulate understandings of equality. It is almost insensitive to say to the woman who has a mere half hour for lunch that she should demand better treatment from her boss, and that she should get her other co-workers to do the same. It is insensitive because you see in her smile, while she's telling you that she is tired, that she is afraid to question her job in case she would be without it, and I can't guarantee her that she will be secure in doing so. Many immigrant workers in Chicago are trapped in fear between asserting their rights and the idea of being replaced and unable to find work. This sort of unspoken oppression and inequality is not easy to define or solve as an issue.

I hope that the members of this class, which is one of thousands, will recognize and use their rights to demand the equality to which they are entitled. Citizenship classes should not be about producing individuals who have memorized answers but about producing individuals, families, and communities who are encouraged and supported in exercising the rights and privileges that they have come to understand exist for everyone.

Index

Acculturation
  relationship to cancer risk, 46
  relationship to substance abuse, 45
Addams, Jane, 135
Adolescents
  African-American, high school
    dropout rate of, 43
  drug abuse by, 45
  educational attainment of, effect of
    poverty on, 42-44
Affirmative action
  African Americans' attitudes
    toward, 162
  Latinos' attitudes toward, 160,
    162,163-164
  opposition to, 48
African American(s)
  attitude toward affirmative action, 162
  citizenship of, 7
  competitive relationship with
    Latinos, 23
  educational attainment, relationship
    to poverty rate, 38,39,40
  as elected officials, 48
  enslavement of, 5,7,8
  income disparity with Anglo
    Americans, 65
  lack of health insurance coverage
    for, 68
  occupational patterns of, 36
  poverty rate of, 30
  segregation of, 3
  voting behavior of, 48
African-American adolescents, high
  school dropout rate of, 43
African-American children,
  educational attainment, effect
  of poverty on, 42
African-American infants,
  low-birth-weight, 44

African-American population,
  comparison with Latino
  population, 2
Agricultural Research Act, 17
AIDS (acquired immunodeficiency
  syndrome), 45-46
Aid to Families with Dependent
  Children (AFDC), 41
Alianza Hispano Americana, 132-133
Alternative learning centers, 51-52
Amalgamated Clothing Workers of
  America, 135
Americas Watch, 110-111
Antiterrorism and Effective Death
  Penalty Act, 12
Arizona, annexation by United States,
  8-9
Arkansas, English-language policy of,
  18
Asia, as U.S. immigration source, 4
Asians. *See also* specific national and
  ethnic groups
  citizenship of, 7

Baby boom generation, retirement of,
  47
Balanced Budget Act of 1997, 16-17
Balseros, 11
Baylor University, 68
Bilingual education, 137
  government funding of, Latinos'
    support for, 160,162
  historical background of, 19
  opposition to, 19-20
Bilingual Education Act of 1968, 19
Bilingualism, 17
Black Congressional Caucus, 56
Border, Mexico-U.S., militarization of,
  12-13

   173

For Product Safety Concerns and Information please contact our EU representative GPSR@taylorandfrancis.com Taylor & Francis Verlag GmbH, Kaufingerstraße 24, 80331 München, Germany

T - #0046 - 270225 - C0 - 212/152/11 [13] - CB - 9780789011602 - Gloss Lamination